The Land Conservancy of McHenry County

2013 Photo Contest

Art of the Land Amateur Photography Contest Catalog

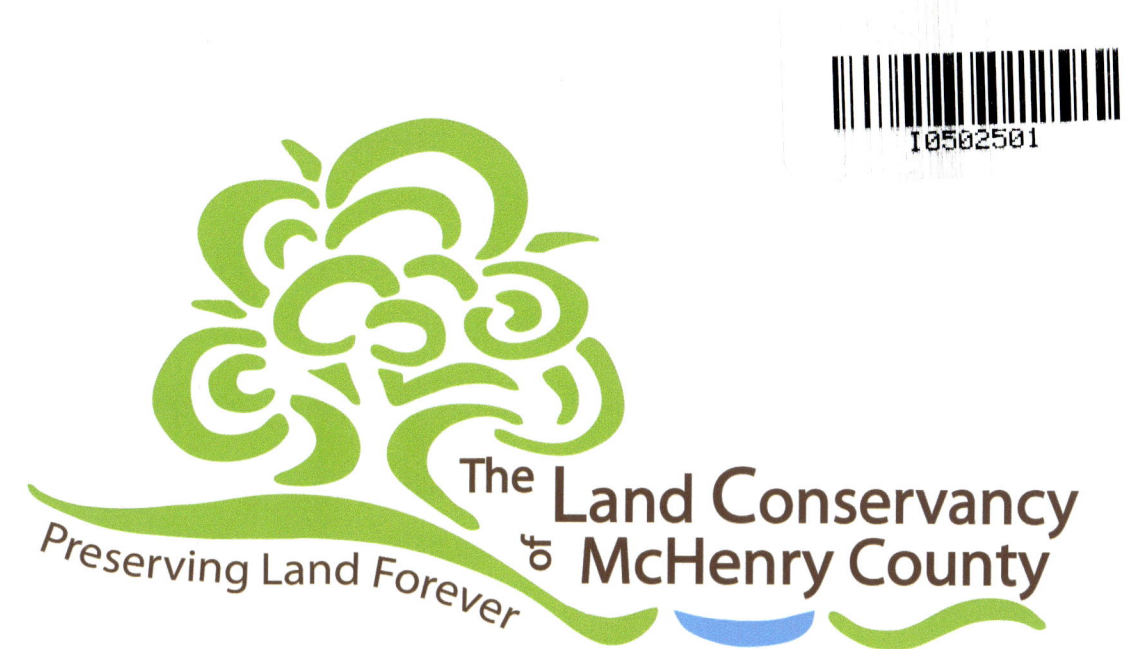

The Land Conservancy of McHenry County

Preserving Land Forever

Our Mission:

To preserve natural, agricultural, and scenic land in perpetuity in and around McHenry County by working with individuals, communities and other partners.

Our Vision:

The Land Conservancy of McHenry County (TLC) will be a respected voice for local land and water resources and for the contributions of private landowners to ensure that future generations will benefit from the natural, agricultural, and scenic landscapes of all scales that residents enjoy today.

McHenry County will be known for its permanently preserved biologically diverse and irreplaceable natural landscapes, scenic vistas that reveal glacial and agricultural heritage of the area, and its strong community support for conservation. A diverse and growing membership and volunteer base will work effectively alongside staff to nurture and expand the conservation community.

About The Land Conservancy of McHenry County:

TLC has worked with nearly 100 landowners to preserve over 2,000 acres of land across McHenry County. Protected properties range from less than 1 acre to 250 acres in size. Preserved lands include high quality wetland and woodland habitat, farmland, scenic vistas, historic farmsteads, and similar valuable land resources.

The organization accomplishes most of its land preservation work by working with individuals who donate permanent conservation restrictions (also called conservation easements) on their land. Occasionally, individuals donate land to TLC and, on rare occasions, TLC purchases land.

TLC is a local 501(c)(3) nonprofit organization recognized by the IRS and the State of Illinois since 1991. The organization is funded by members, grants, and fundraising events like Art of the Land.

Acorn Lane Conservation Area, Lake in the Hills
3rd Place Winner

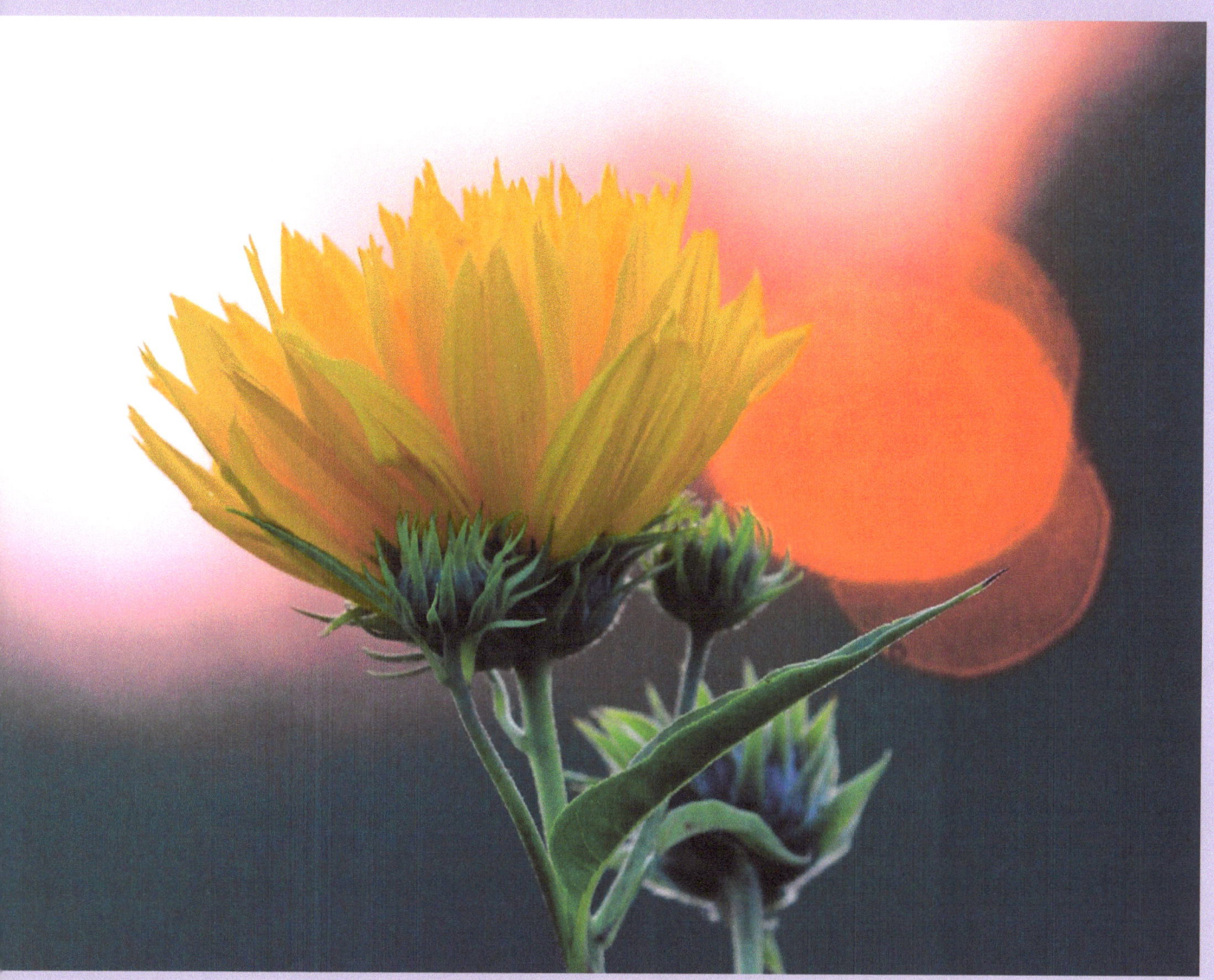

Photographer: Paul McFadden
13 Acres donated to TLC in 2006

This preserve protects a section of Woods Creek and the surrounding wetland, allowing it to stay natural in a densely developed area. Now, animals of all sorts have a nice home in Lake in the Hills.

Anderson Conservation Easement, Nunda Township
Honorable Mention and People's Choice Winner

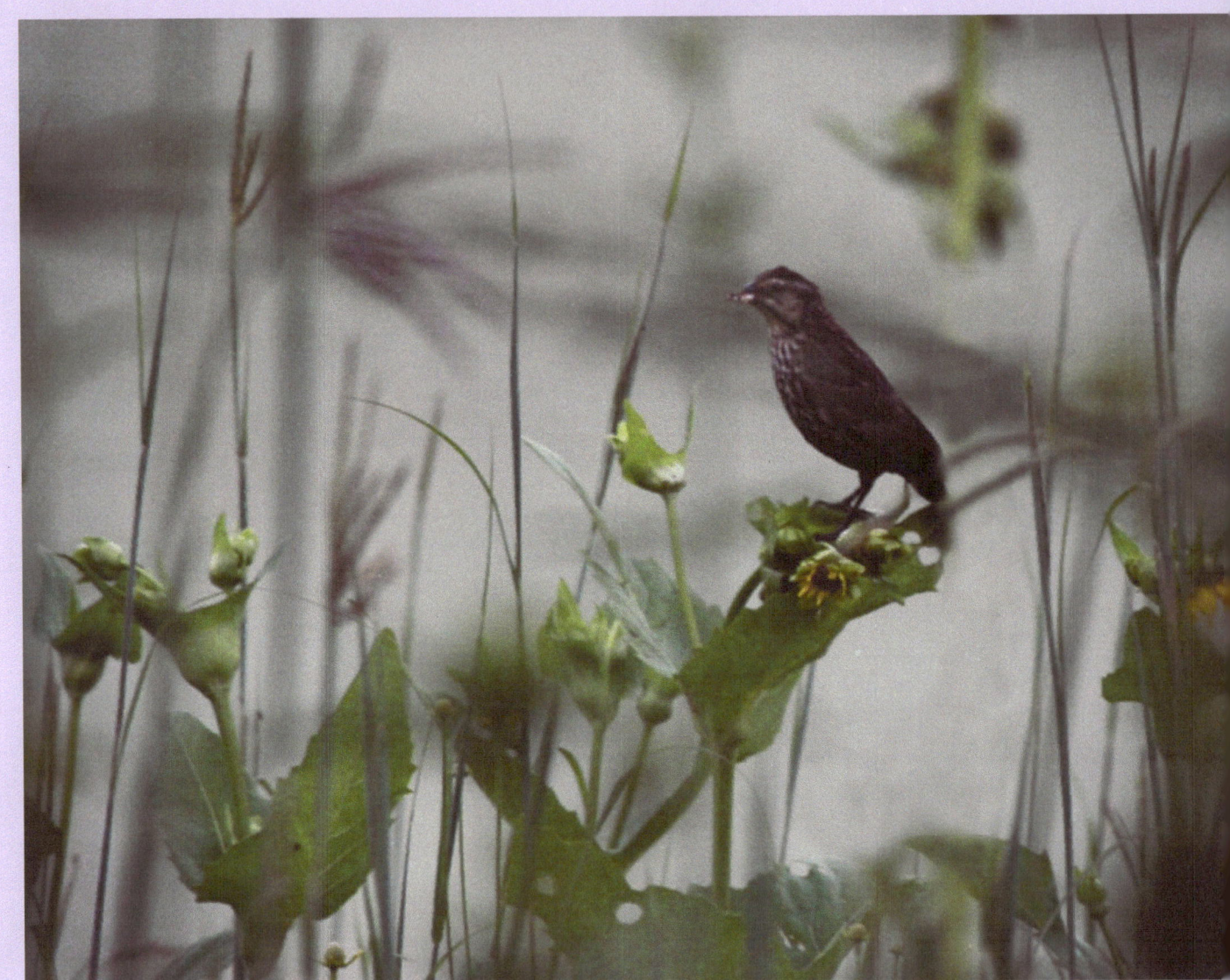

Photographer: Cate Welk
2 Acres dedicated to TLC in 1994

The Andersons were some of the first people in the county to place a voluntary easement on their land, helping to provide incentive for preservation of the Powers Creek watershed. On the easement, paths lead through their backyard, ducking around ponds, under trees, and through patches of native prairie plants.

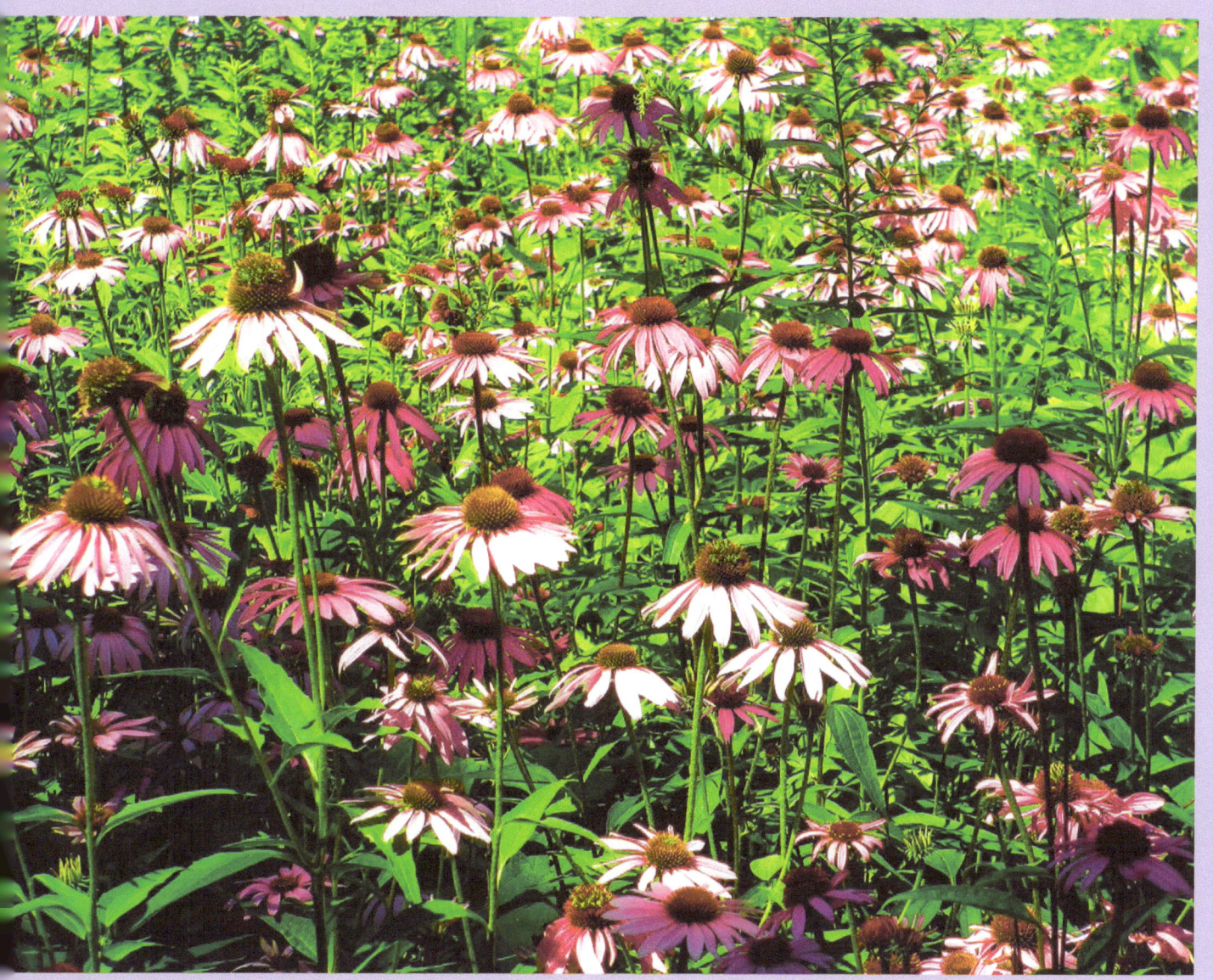

Photographer: Karl Krause
11 Acres dedicated to TLC in 2009

Don and Dorothy Arvidson own a wonderful piece of land with tall, majestic, remnant oaks that likely were here to see European settlers arriving in the area. Because of their hard work, these oaks are protected and will hopefully be looking down on us for another couple hundred years.

Bangert Conservation Easement, Alden

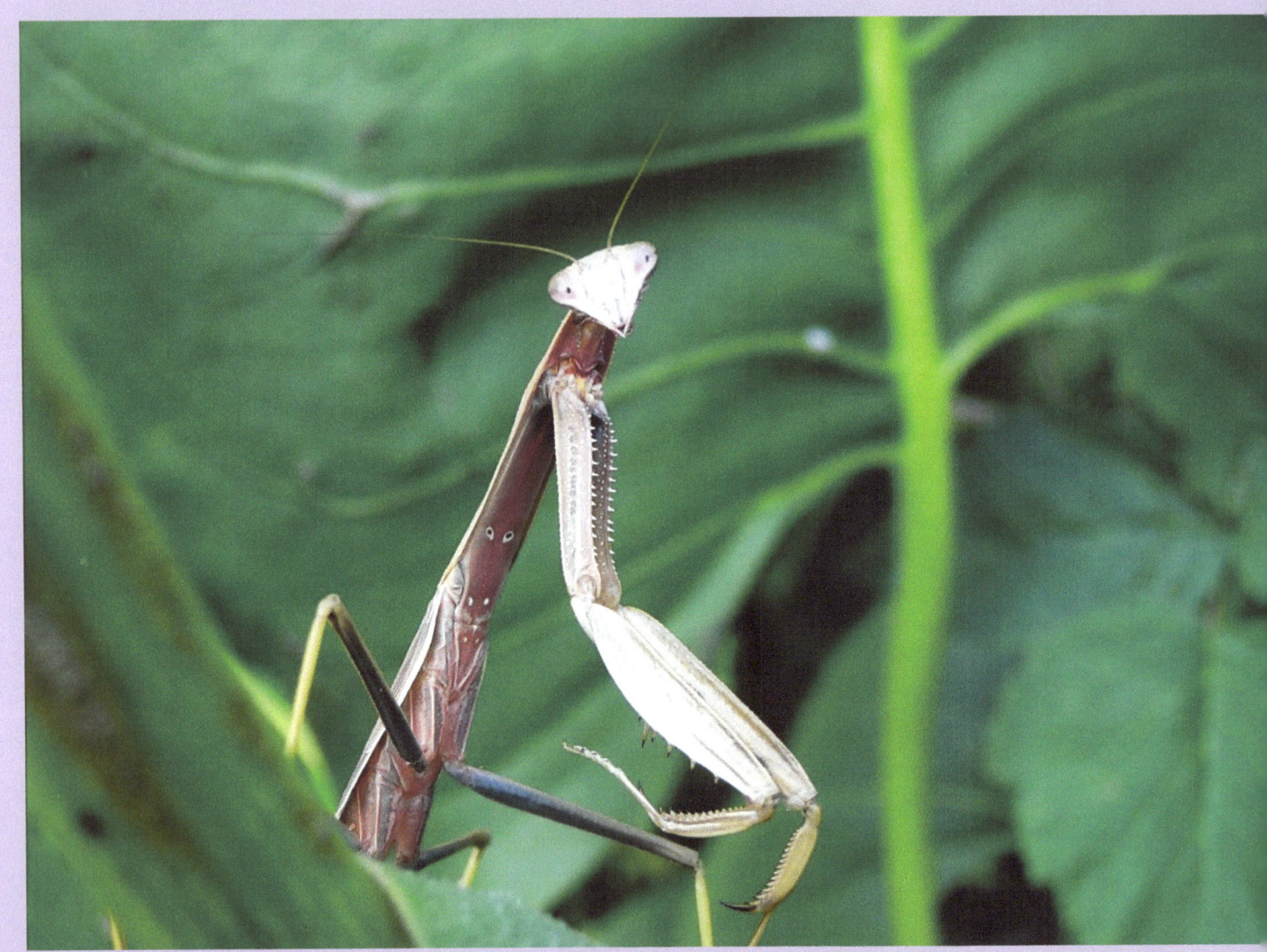

Photographer: Corie Stevens
17 Acres dedicated to TLC in 2009

Orrin and Patricia Bangert have been instrumental in conserving the natural areas around the "High Point" in McHenry County (1189 feet above sea level). When they placed a conservation easement on their property, it brought attention to the area and eventually resulted in the Conservation District purchasing 253 neighboring acres.

Bangert Conservation Easement, Alden

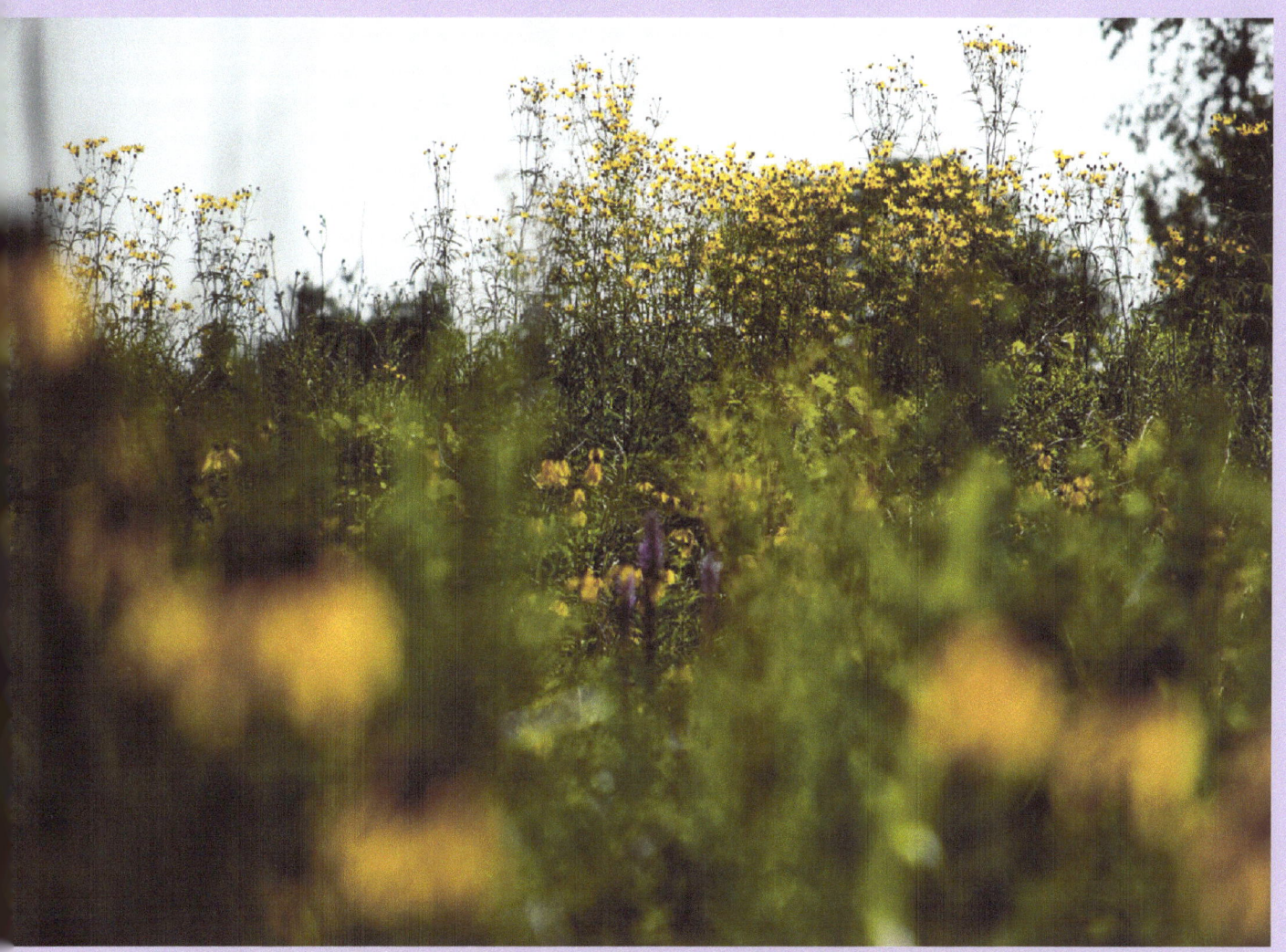

Photographer: Elizabeth Tanner
17 Acres dedicated to TLC in 2009

The Bangert's dedication and pride show when you look around their property which abounds with blooming wildflowers and native grasses. The wet areas on this land provide great turtle, frog and salamander habitat. Orrin and Patricia have helped spread the restoration land ethic through the region by hosting an annual seed sharing day.

Beeson Conservation Easement, Harvard

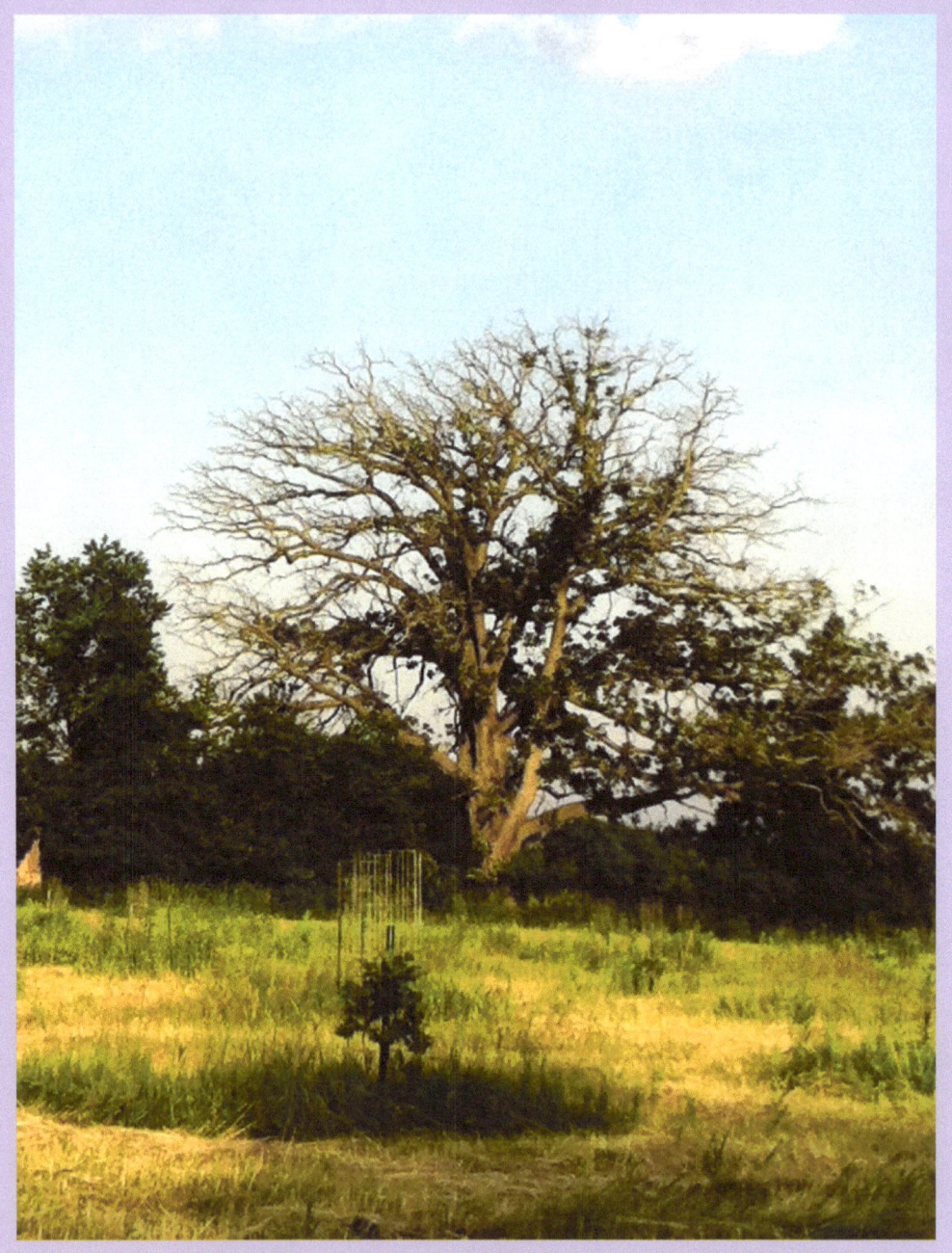

Photographer: Mary McClelland
130 Acres dedicated to TLC in 2009

We were very excited at TLC when this easement was dedicated since it was our first in Chemung Township! This vast area of land features an ancient oak woods, gently rolling landforms, and a large wetland complex.

Bothie Conservation Easement, Woodstock

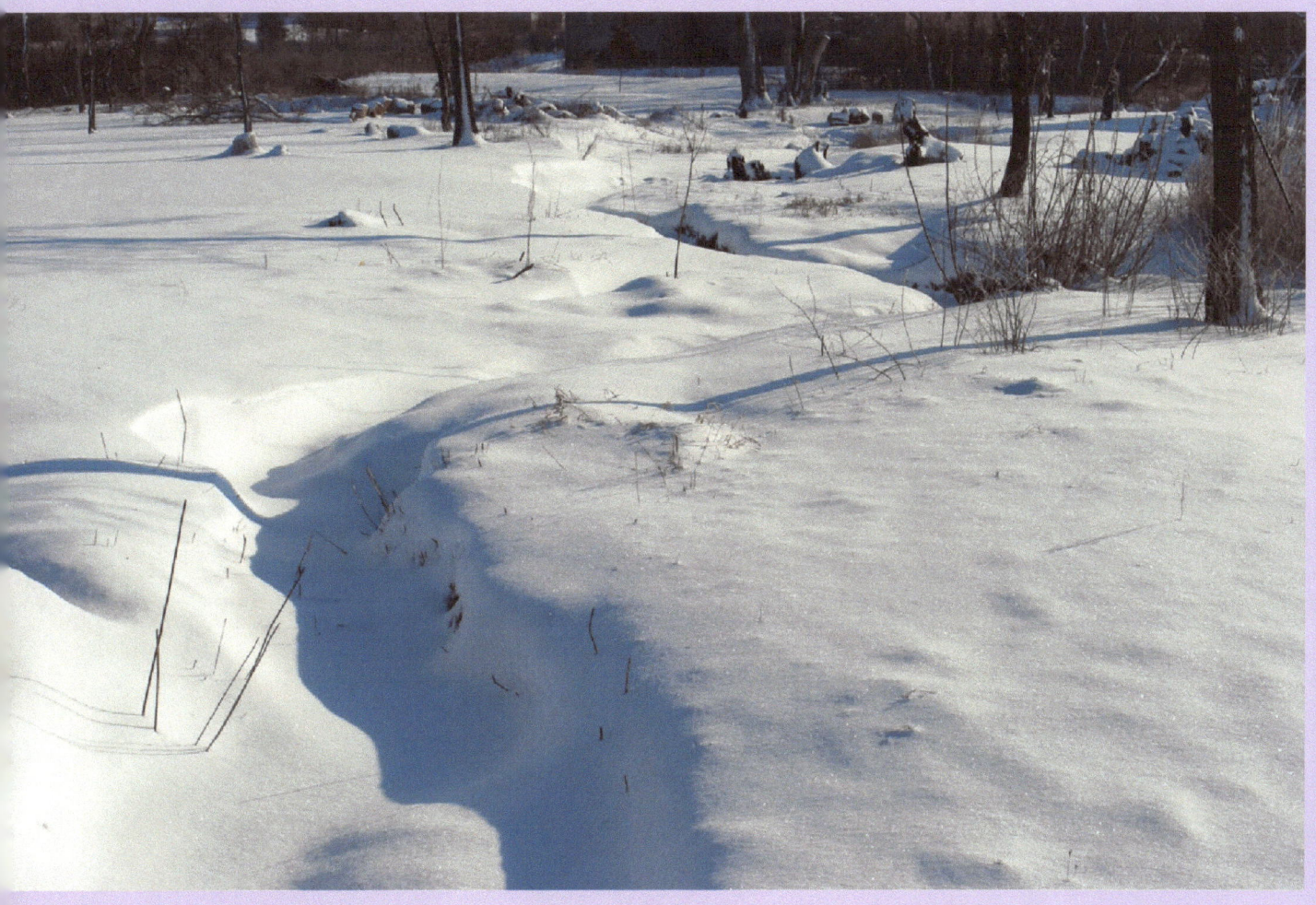

Photographer: Al Edlund
39 Acres dedicated to TLC in 2011

Landowners Teresa Krafcisin and Ray Goder can wake up and watch cranes landing in their wetland or spot foxes or deer trotting by. That's why they chose to name their easement "The Bothie"- a Scottish word meaning a place to stop and rest when weary. This applies to both animals and people!

Brookdale/Woodstock Center Conservation Easemen
Dunham Township

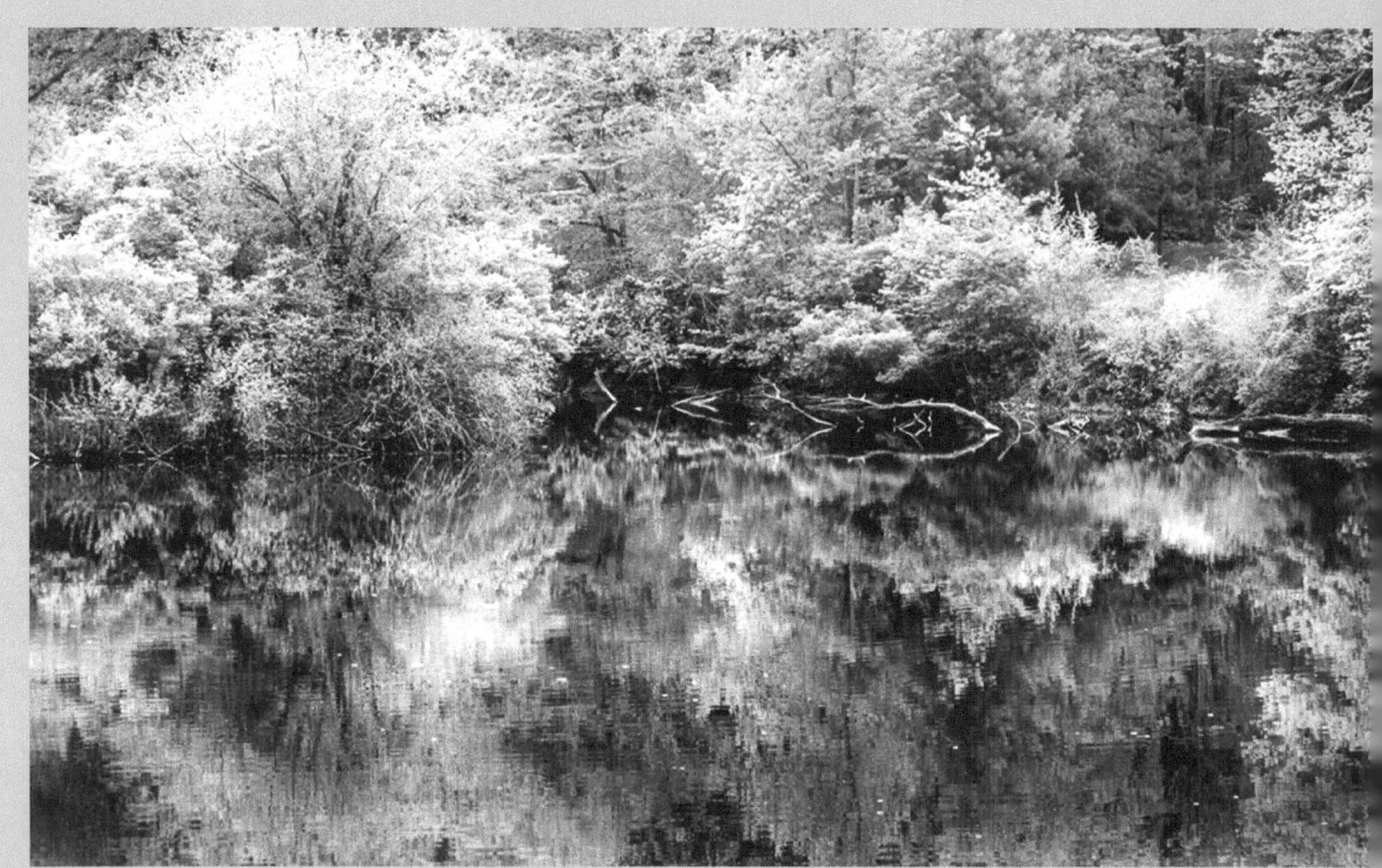

Photographer: Gail Moreland
65 Acres dedicated to TLC in 1999

The Woodstock Center easement was donated to TLC by the Scheinfeld family at the same time the property was sold to McHenry County Conservation District. The property forms the nucleus for what has now become a 1,200+ acre public conservation area.

Colonel Holcomb Estates Conservation Easement, Nunda Township

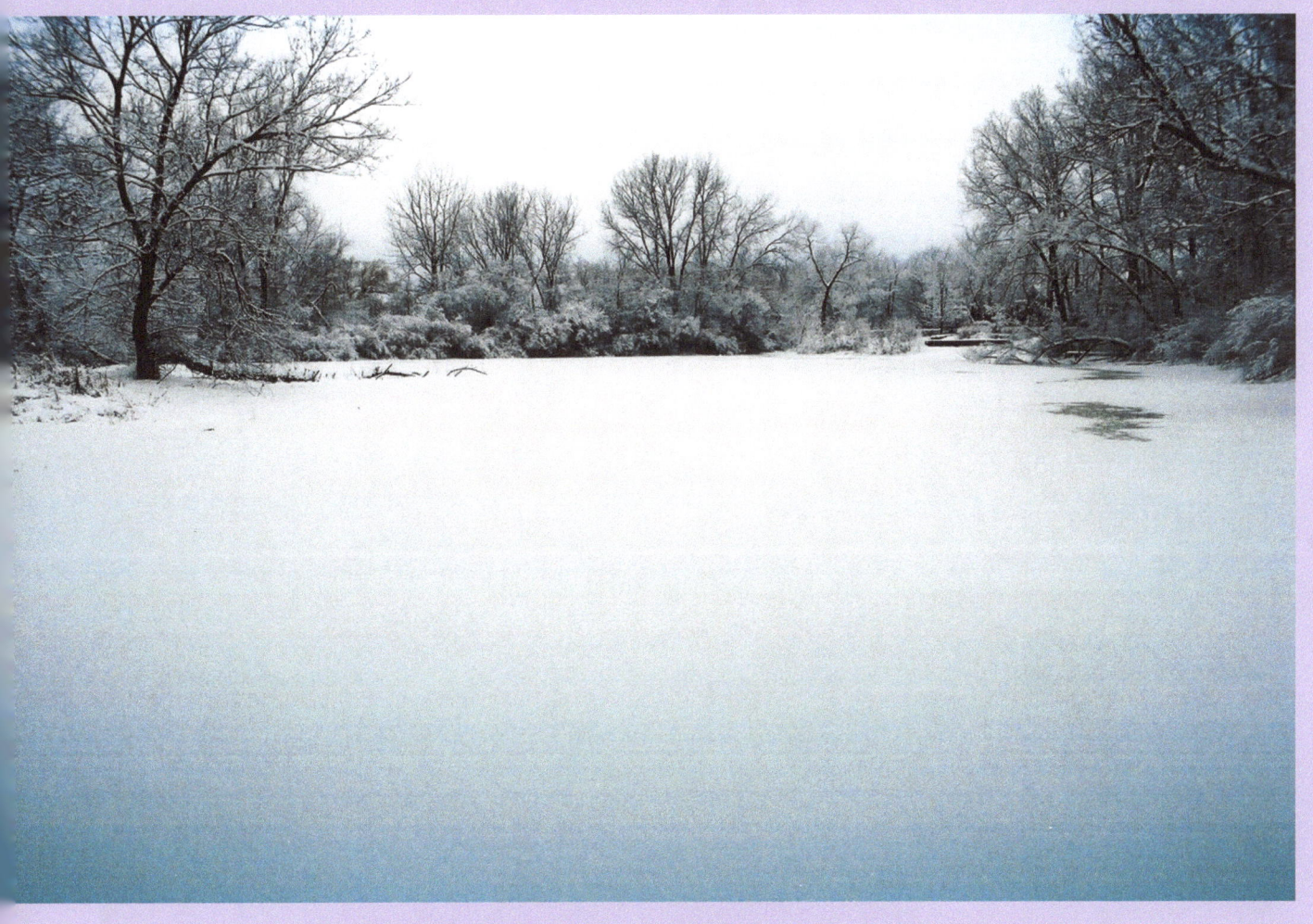

Photographer: Kristin Kellett
5 Acres dedicated to TLC in 1995

This easement is part of a development designed to protect water quality and natural resources. Wetlands and an oak woodland are preserved now, and the residents can appreciate nature being part of their neighborhood.

Concannon Conservation Area, Woodstock

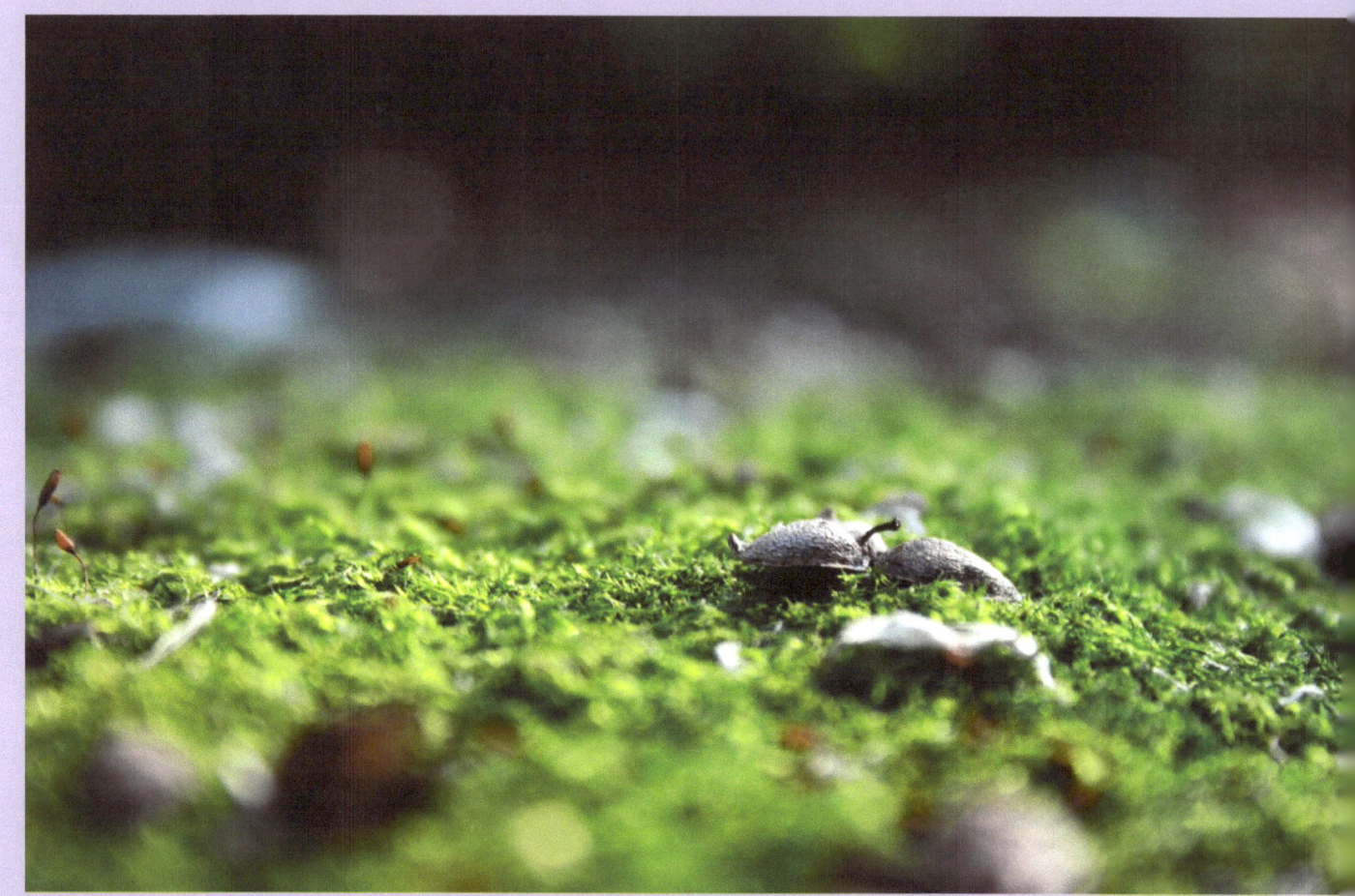

Photographer: Zakary Myshkowec
2 Acres donated to TLC in 2011

On a little street corner in Woodstock was a forgotten parcel of land. Muriel Concannon decided that since she didn't have plans to use it, she would dedicate it to The Land Conservancy. Since then, we've been working away at clearing the invasive species, and have been rewarded with finding beautiful native plants that have been waiting for years for someone to care for them!

Crowley Sedge Meadow, Alden

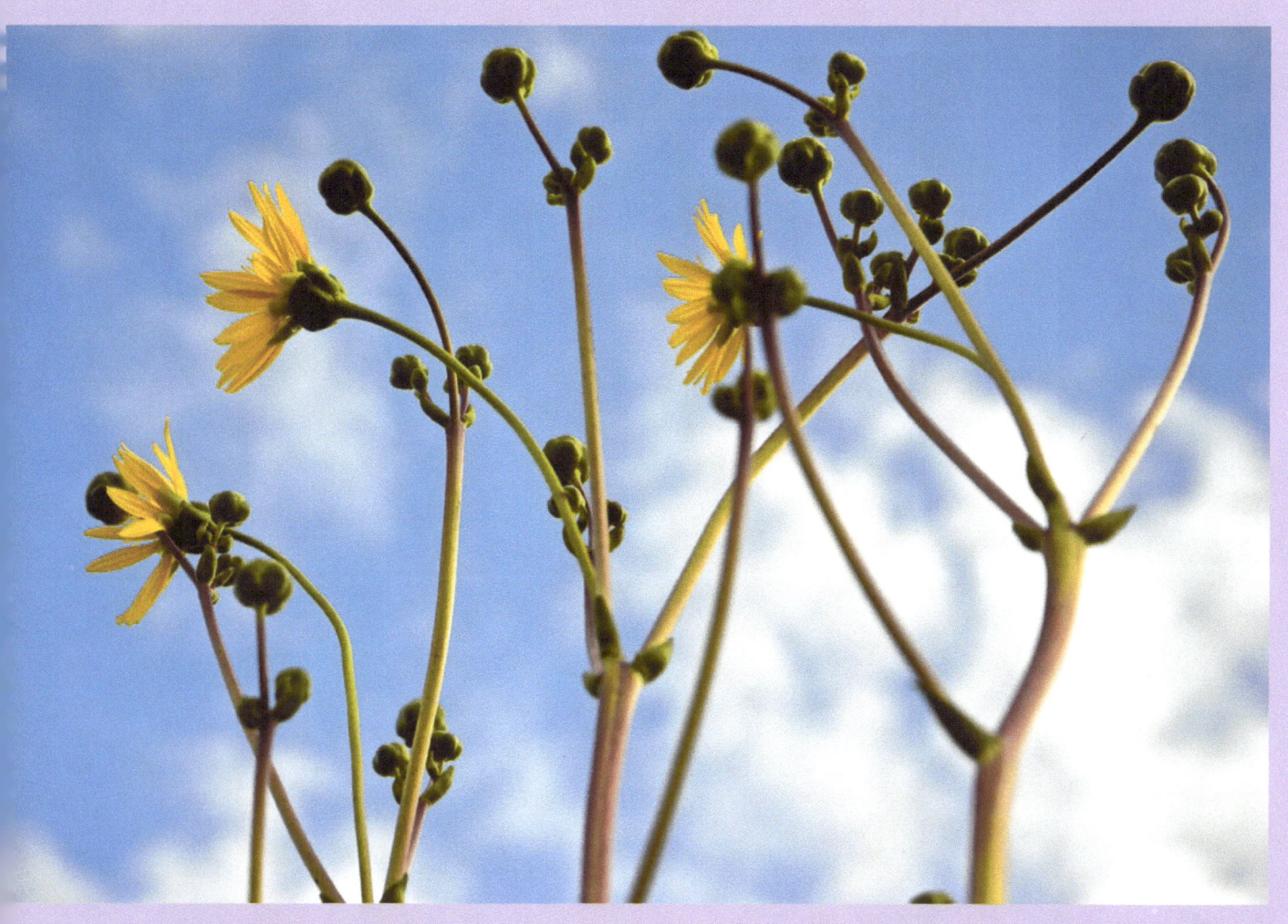

Photographer: Debra Oldham
6.7 Acres purchased by TLC in 2004

Crowley Sedge Meadow is the first land purchased by TLC, protecting this small remnant natural area that was too small for a government agency to acquire. This site proves that sometimes the best things come in small packages!

Crowley Sedge Meadow, Alden

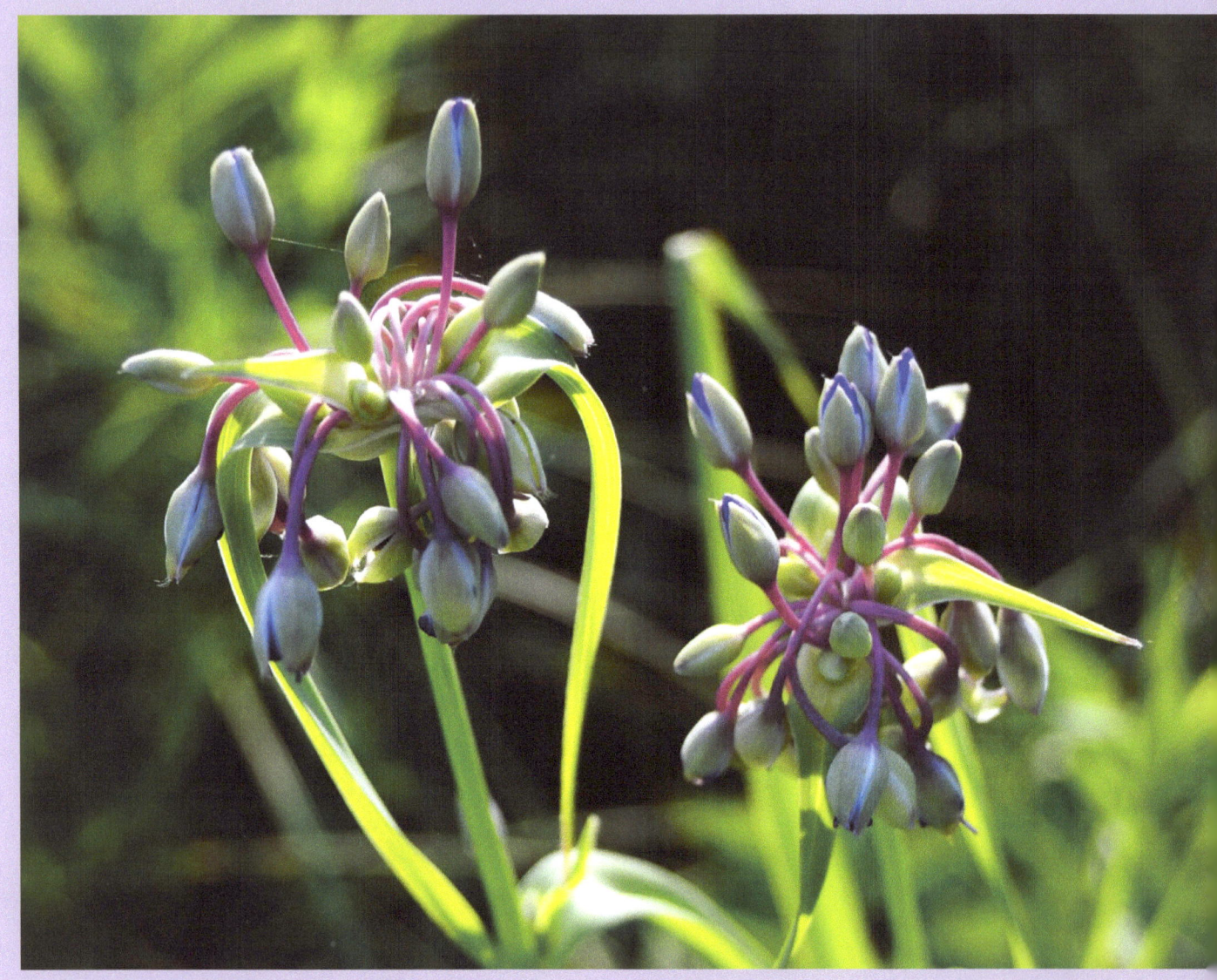

Photographer: Rob Peterson
6.7 Acres purchased by TLC in 2004

Many volunteer hours have gone towards brush clearing, weed
pulling, prescribed fires, and oak plantings.
This little sedge meadow really shines now!

Dutch Creek Conservation Easement, Johnsburg

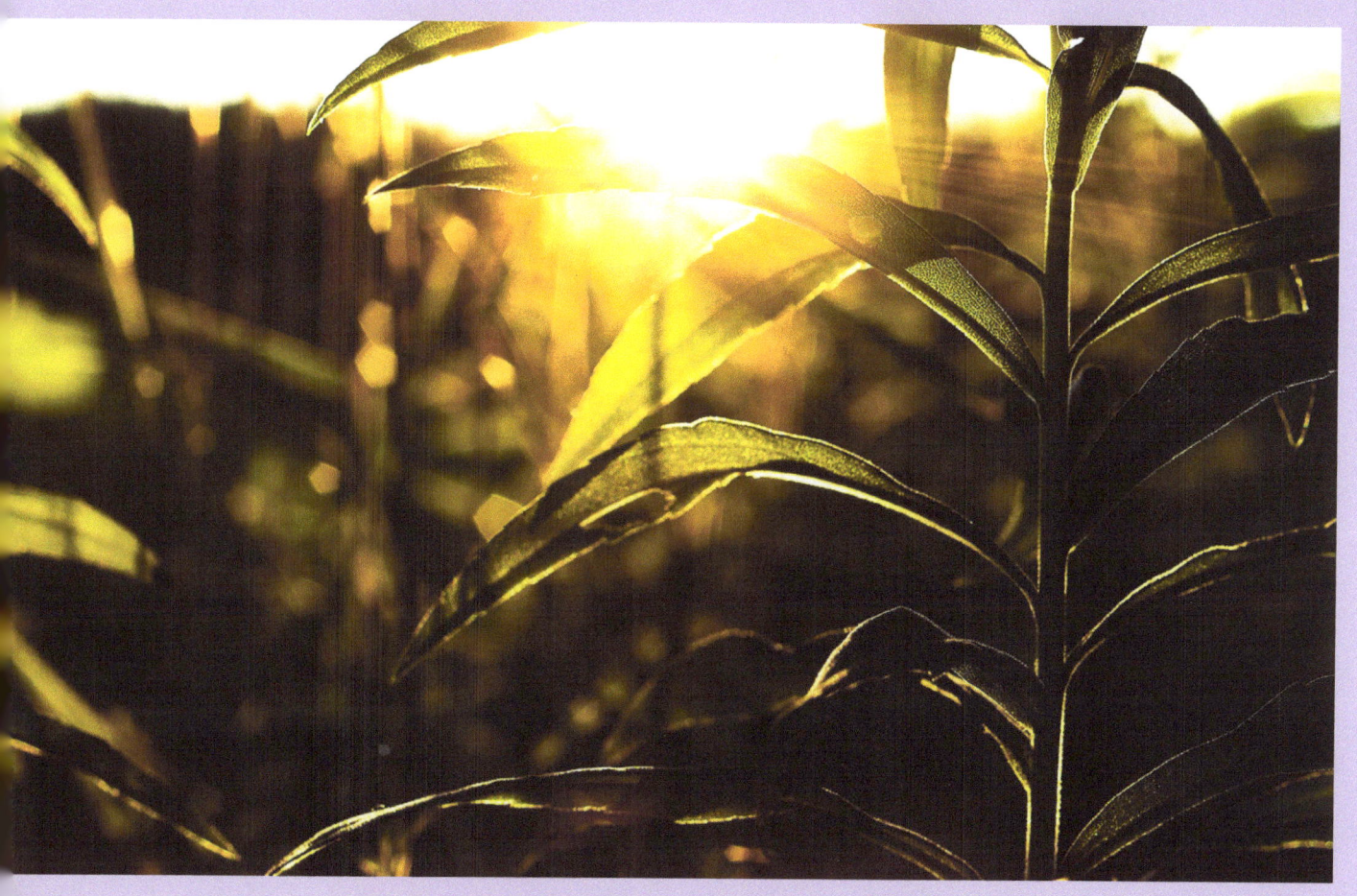

Photographer: Carolyn Bouso
60 Acres dedicated to TLC in 2007

This easement, located within the Dutch Creek Estates subdivision, is part of a larger complex of land protected by TLC, the Conservation District, and the village of Johnsburg. By working together with other organizations, we can protect the 170 native plant species that call this their home.

Dutch Creek Conservation Easement, Johnsburg

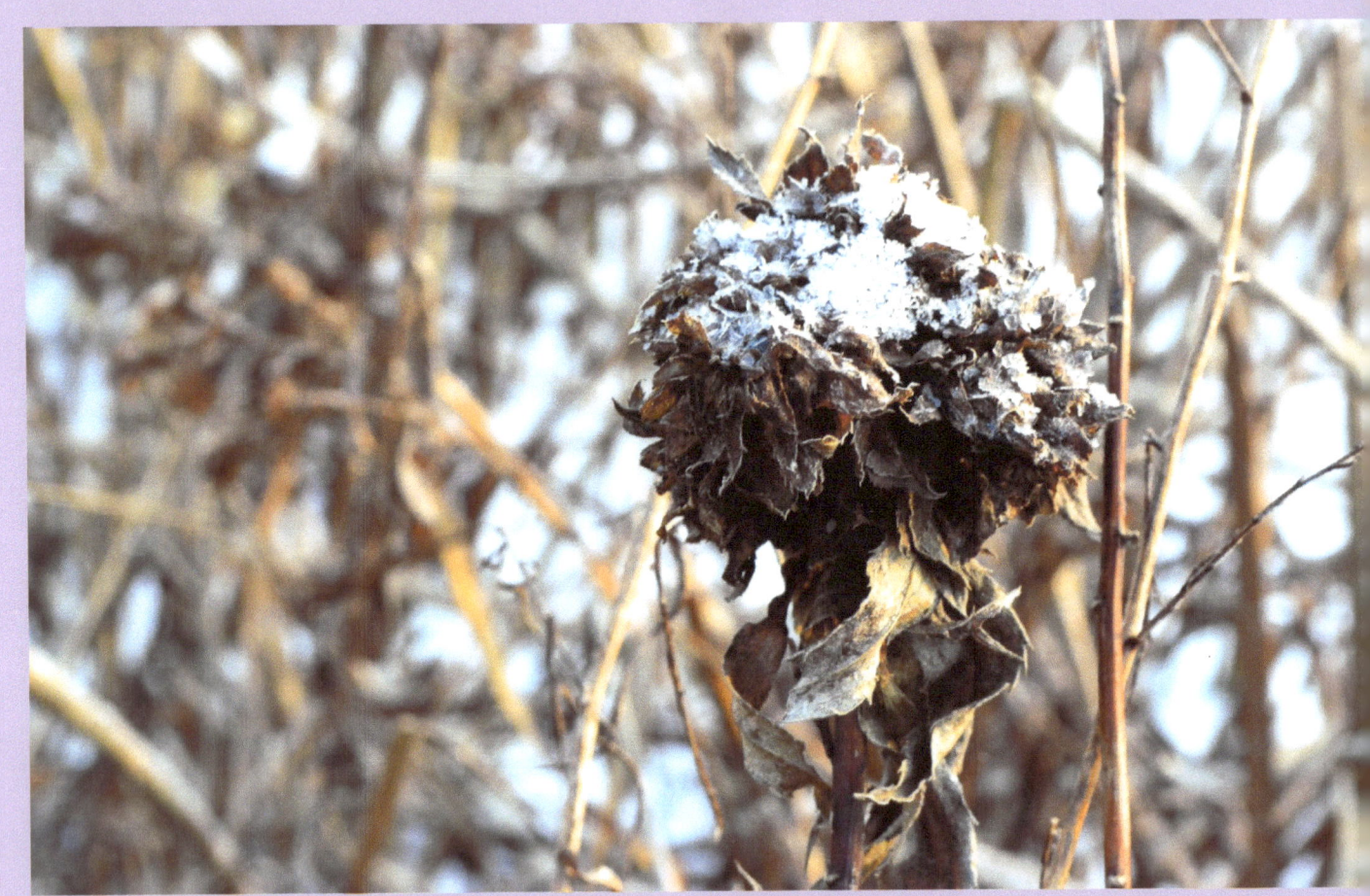

Photographer: Valerie Bouso
60 Acres dedicated to TLC in 2007

This easement includes one of the highest quality headwater streams in the county- Dutch Creek. The stream flows through sedge meadows, fens, and oak woodlands.

Dutch Creek Conservation Easement, Johnsburg
Honorable Mention

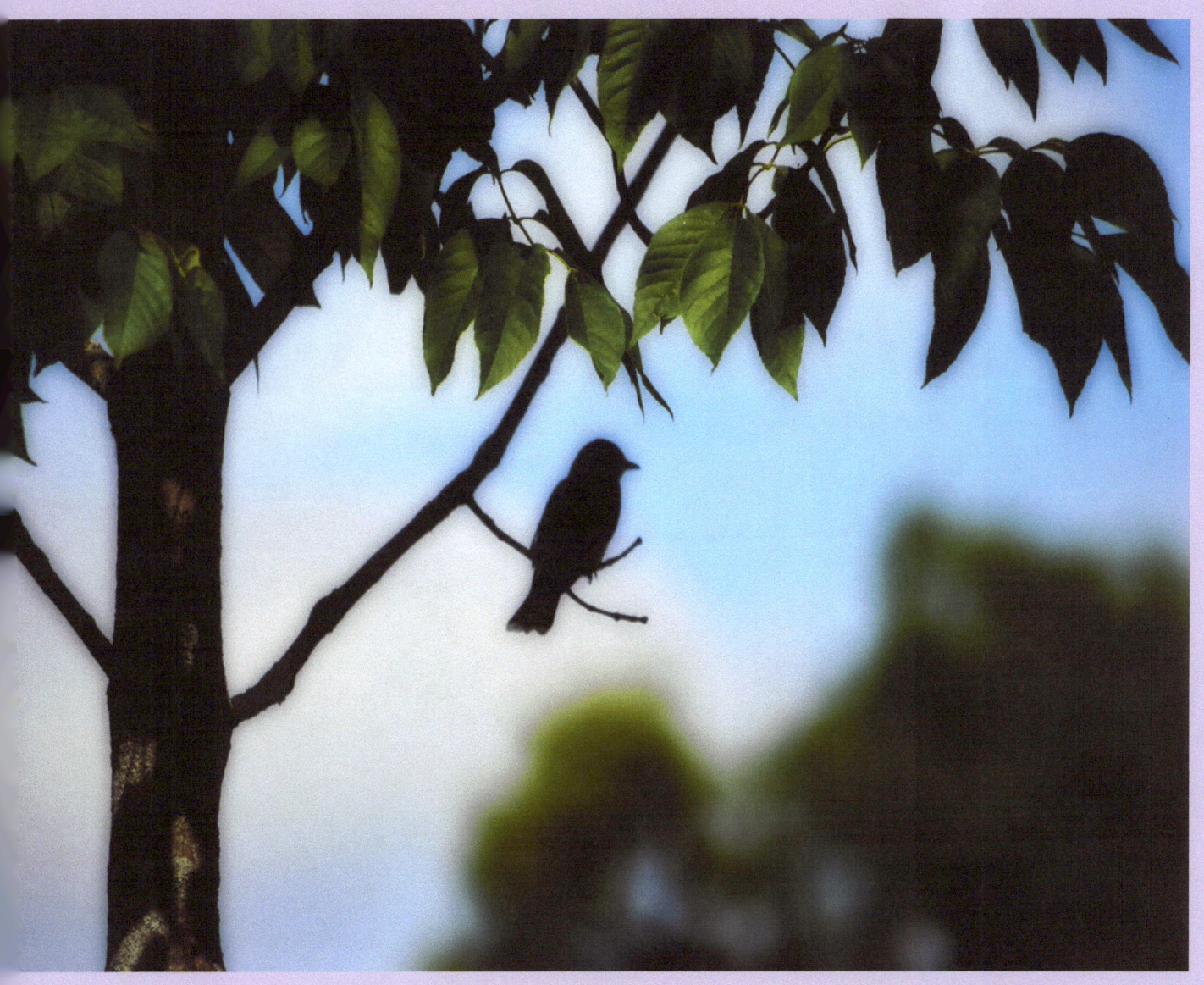

Photographer: Caroline Flaherty
60 Acres dedicated to TLC in 2007

Site steward Bob Roe restores this land, because of "My general love of being outdoors and tackling physical challenges, my desire to contribute to creating as healthy an environment as possible for humankind and all living creatures, and my hope to nurture a spirit of caring for the land in my community that will inspire future generations to continue this journey."

Ericsson-Olson Preserve, McHenry Township

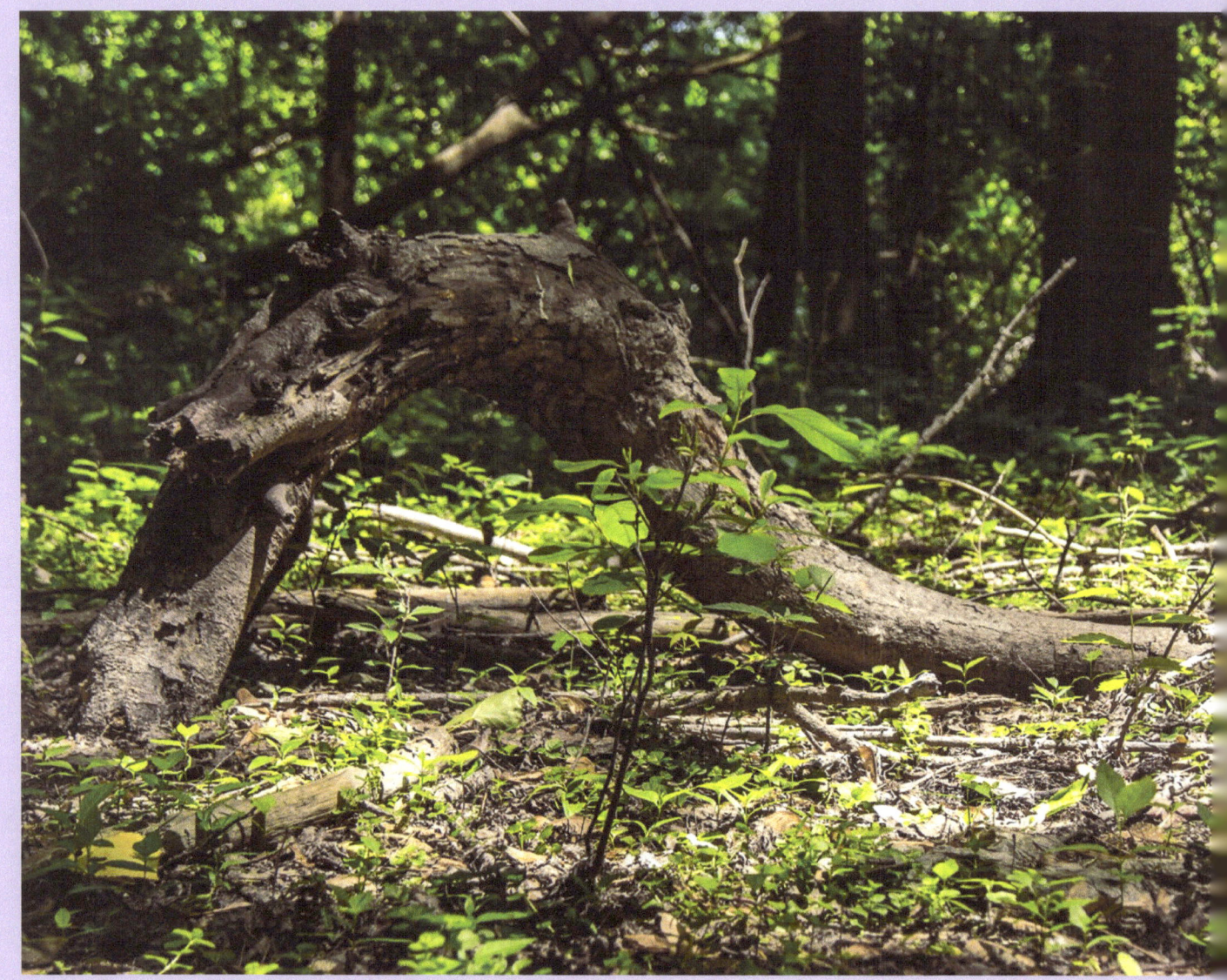

Photographer: Steven Orzech
3 Acres donated to TLC in 2009

This land along Pistakee Lake was in the same family since the 1800s. The three Olson sisters agreed on a donation to TLC, protecting the natural lakeshore and the lagoon in an area where mowed lawns line most of the lake.

Eriksen Conservation Easement, Bull Valley

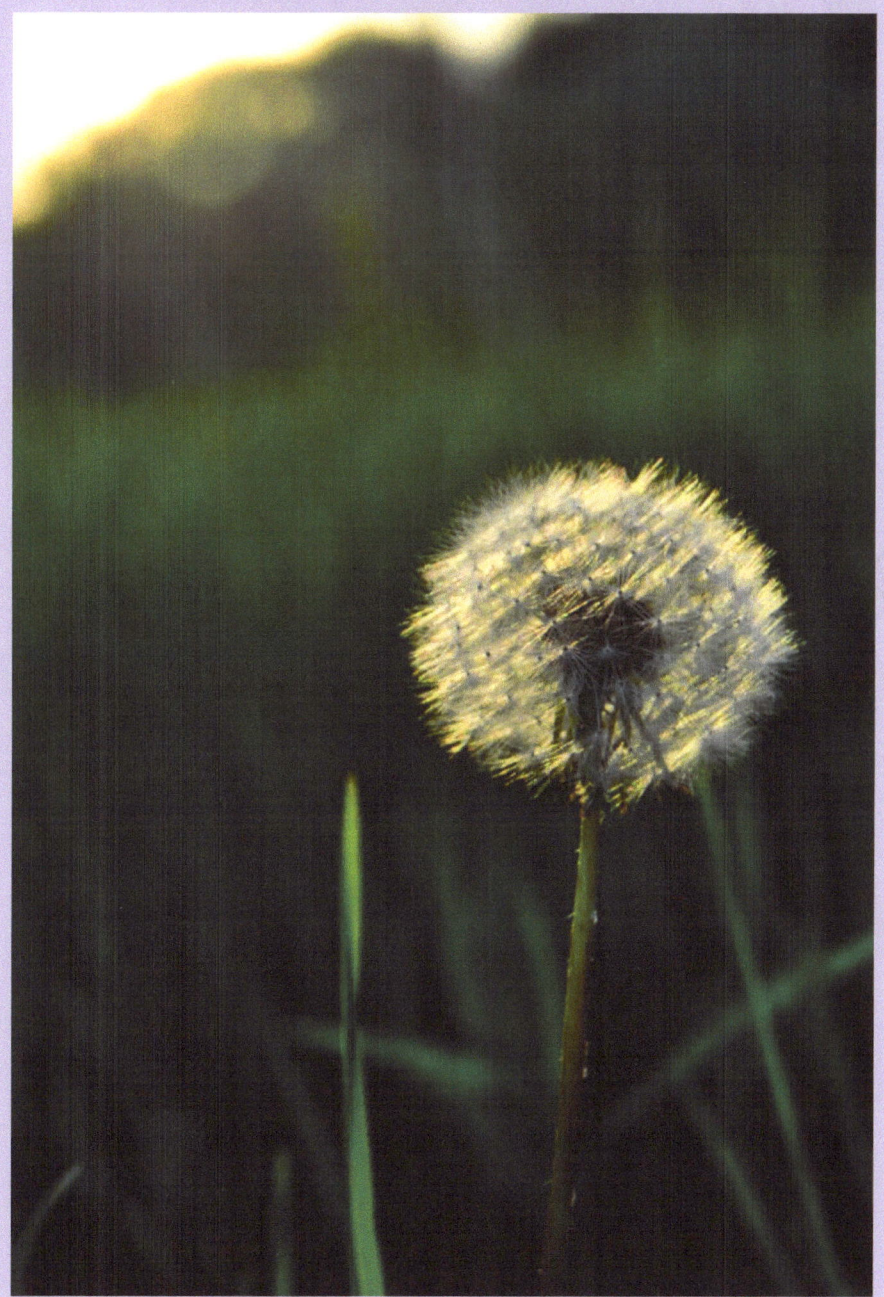

Photographer: Lauren Erickson
10 Acres dedicated to TLC in 2004

This former tree nursery located in "downtown" Bull Valley, where Boone Creek crosses Bull Valley Road, provides an important buffer to the nearby Boone Creek Fen Nature Preserve – one of the rarest, highest quality natural areas in the state. By choosing to permanently protect their property, the Eriksens are helping to ensure that the groundwater resources that feed the fen remain plentiful and clean.

Frisbie Conservation Easement, Woodstock

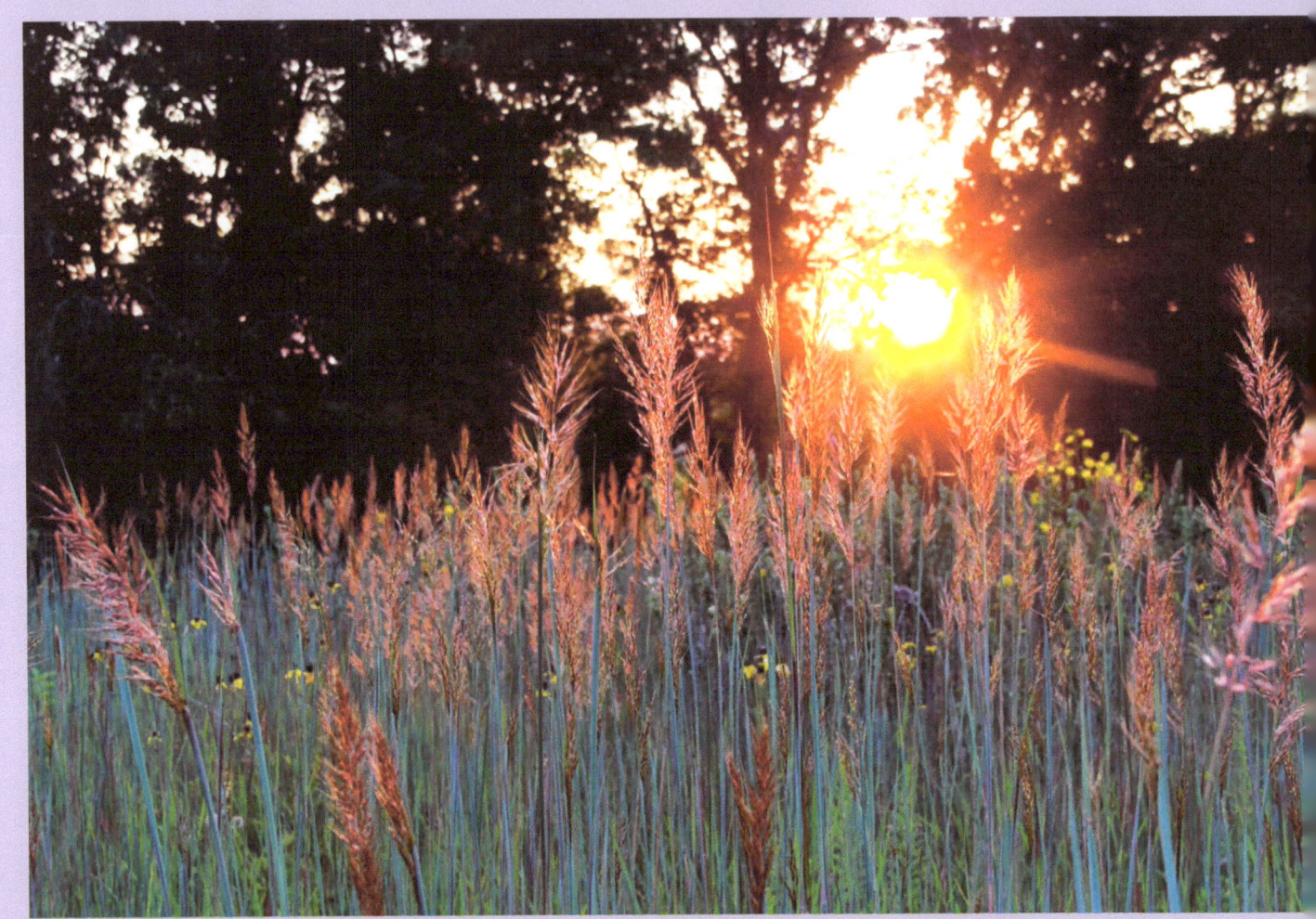

Photographer: Michelle Myshkowec
56 Acres dedicated to TLC in 2011

When this land was purchased in 1993 it was mostly farmland. Now meadows of prairie, wetland, and woodland wildflowers and grasses spread out across the land. The Frisbies have a land ethic that should truly be appreciated. They've served on many environmental organizations' boards across the region, installed super energy-efficient devices in their home, utilize geothermal and solar energy, drive an electric car, and still find time to restore their property. Thanks Marlene and Hugh!

Hennen Conservation Area, Woodstock

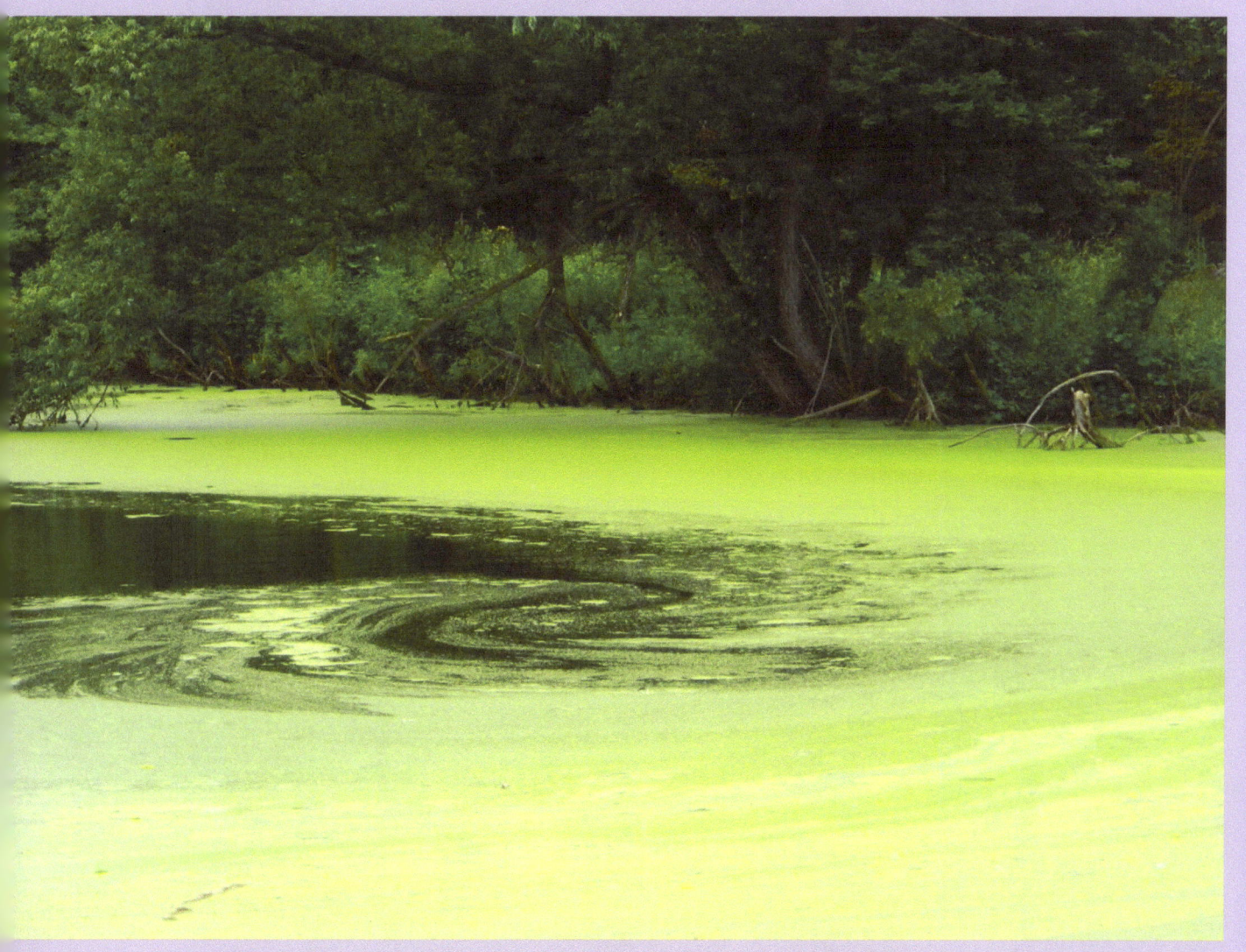

Photographer: Sarah Cashmore
25 Acres dedicated to TLC in 2008

Phyllis and Tony Hennen acquired this land in the early 70s, planting thousands of native hardwood seedlings. In 2008, they placed a conservation easement on the land through TLC. In 2009, they donated the land to the city of Woodstock as a public park, and TLC moved their offices to the farmhouse. Ongoing restoration of the property continues, and we're proud to continue what the Hennens began.

Hidden Marsh Conservation Easement, Hebron

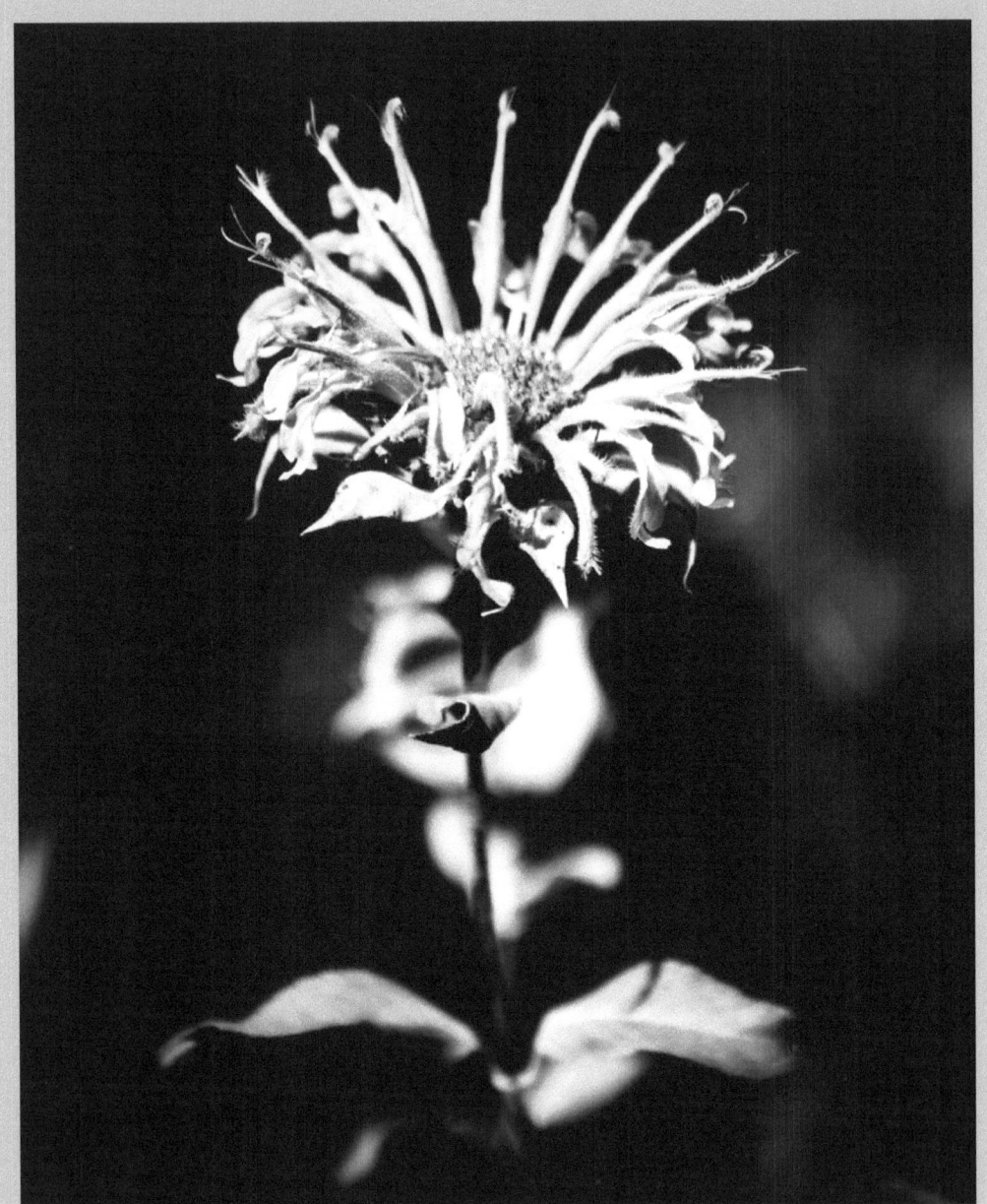

Photographer: Stacy Pahl
20 Acres dedicated to TLC in 2007

Two glacial kames will never be mined for gravel. A sedge meadow will never be filled for development. An oak woodland will never be cleared for a farm field. This is the power of a conservation easement. When David and Joanne first purchased the land, there was so much buckthorn and honeysuckle that it was hard to see the kame, the wetland, and even Wisconsin (just across the property line). They have put in countless hours of work restoring the land. The young oak trees will thank them every day for the next couple hundred years.

Horsefair Springs/1000 Oaks Conservation Easement, Spring Grove

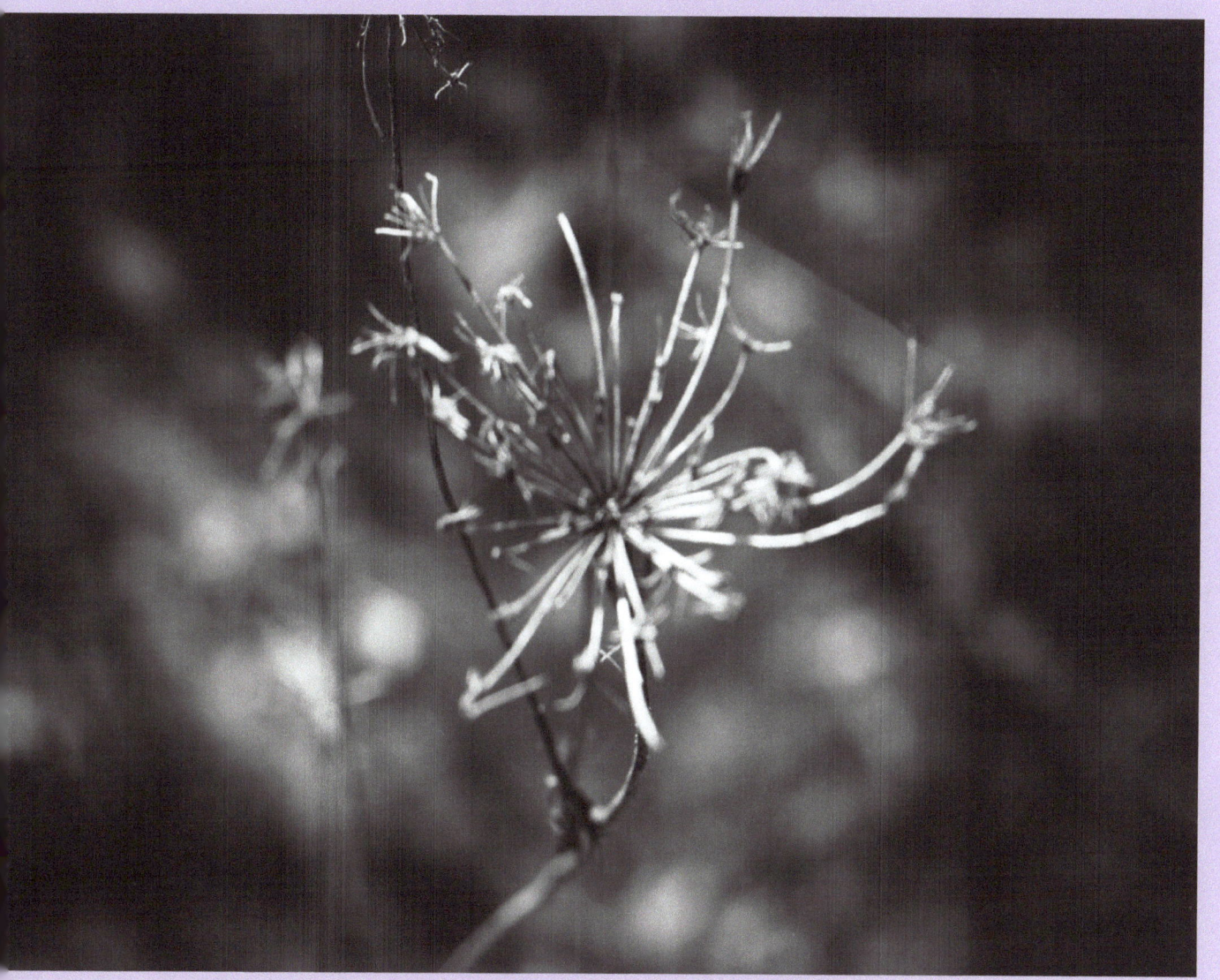

Photographer: Nicole Domanico
9 Acres donated to TLC in 2007

This easement is part of one of the largest, highest quality unprotected wetlands in the county. Located next to the Thousand Oaks subdivision, the easement provides a nice pocket of nature for all the residents so they can appreciate the oak trees and various wildflowers right in their back yards.

Hunter Conservation Easement, Ringwood

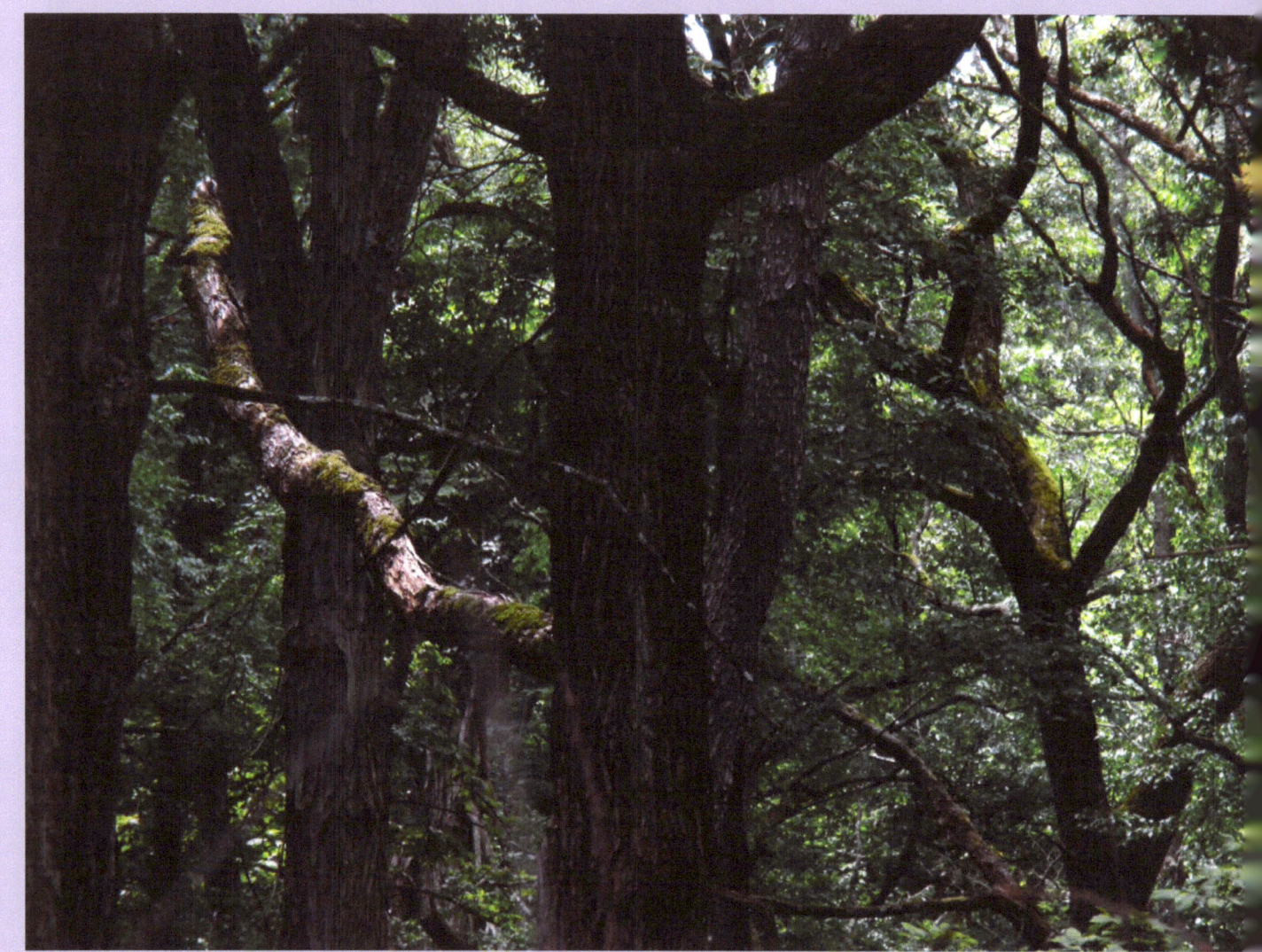

Photographer: Lynn Schiele
14 Acres dedicated to TLC in 2009

The Hunters have ensured this majestic oak woodland will be available for future generations to enjoy, both though a conservation easement and brush clearing restoration efforts. Located next to MCCD's Glacial Park and the Arvidson Conservation Easement, most of this forest is now protected.

Pensinger Conservation Easement, Dorr Township

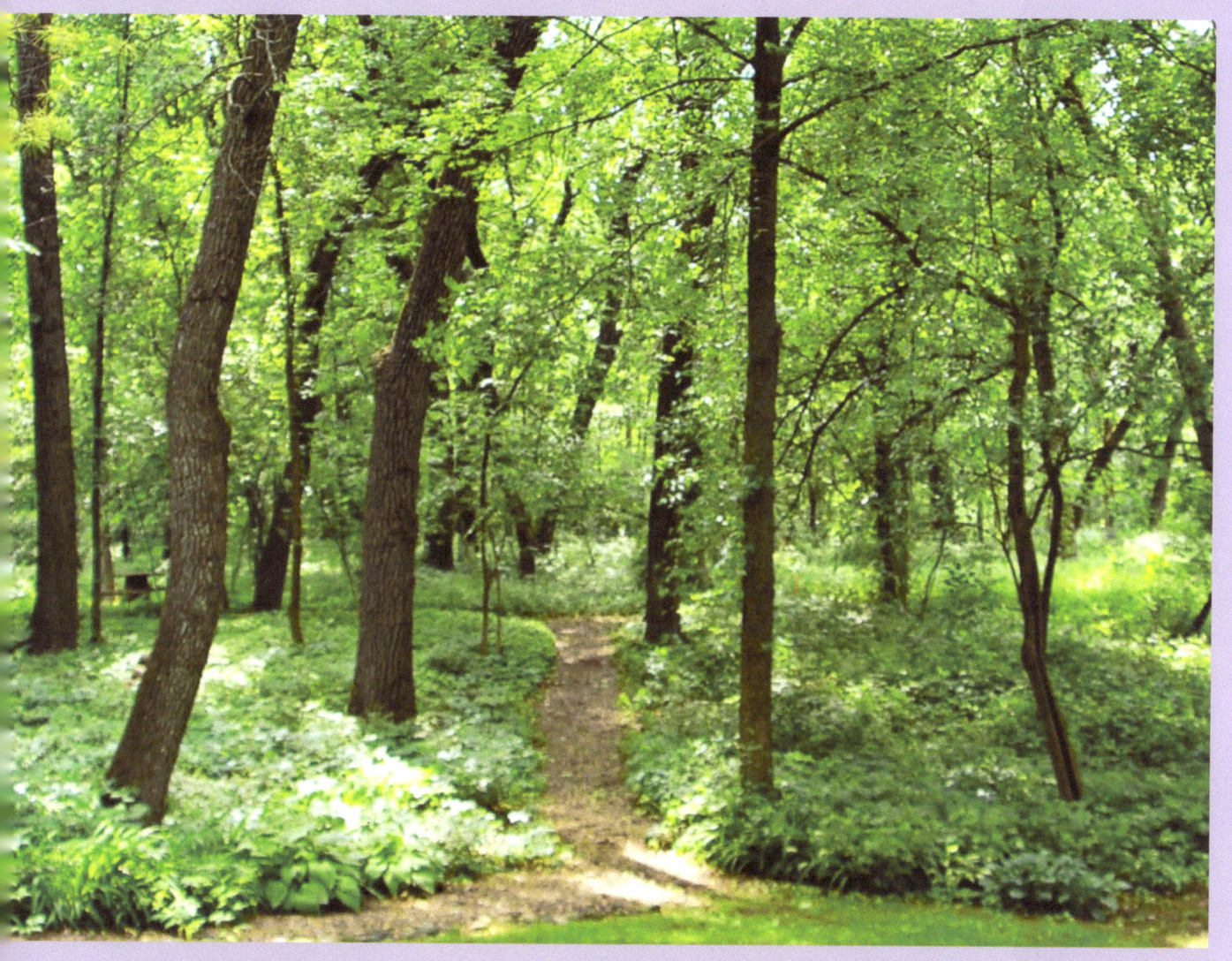

Photographer: Pauline Rucker-White
3.5 Acres dedicated to TLC in 2009

ynn and Ray Pensinger wanted to protect their grove of old hickory and oak trees, and have started clearing the invasive brush from the nderstory. With the increase in light, an abundance of wildflowers have sprung up on the woodland floor.

Queensbury Farm Conservation Easement, Dorr Township

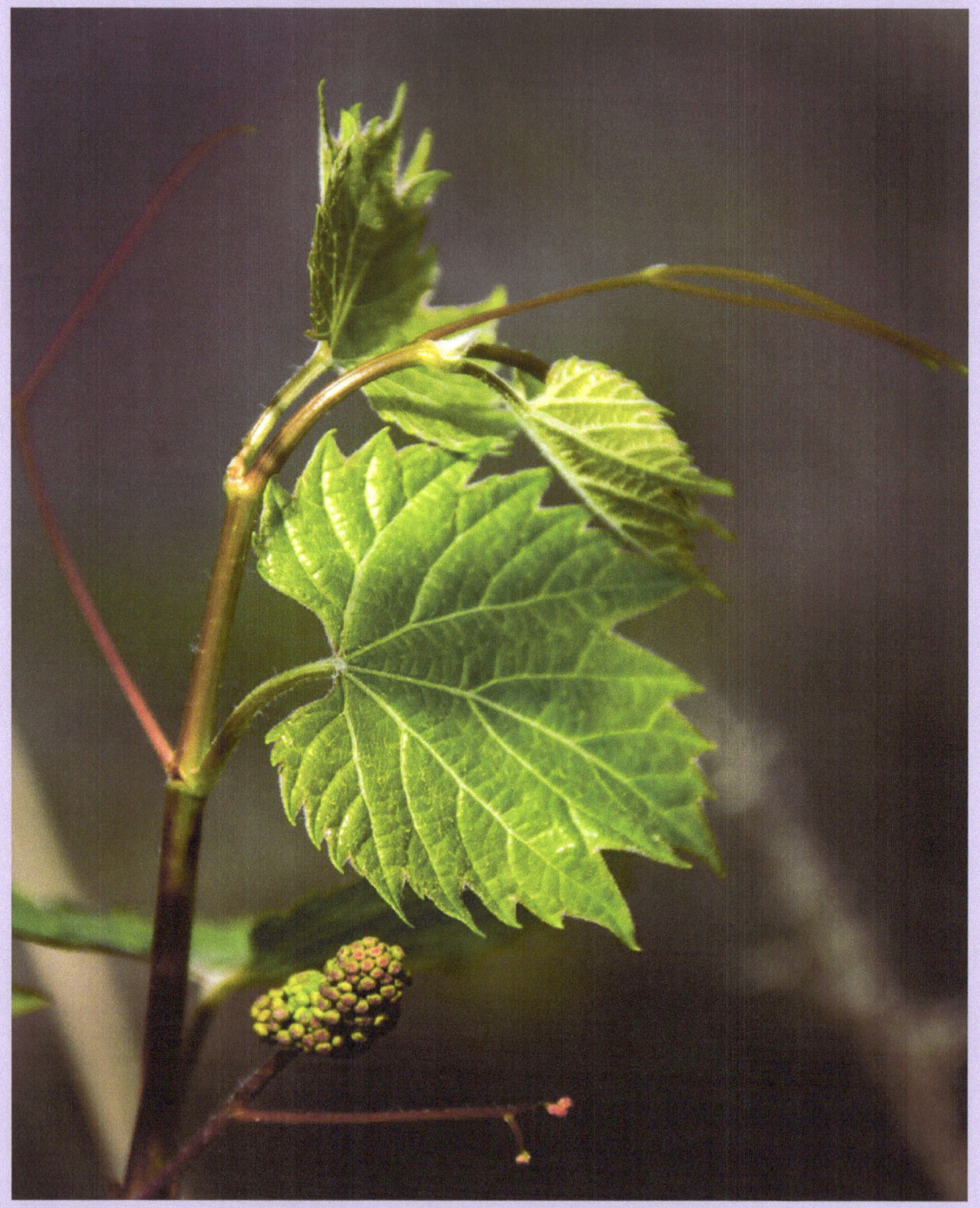

Photographer: Kathy Malecki
35 Acres dedicated to TLC in 2007

When Sue Powers saw the "land for sale" signs go up across the stree[t] from her, she placed her 58 acre property into a conservation easemen[t] to ensure it would never be developed. The slow transformation back t[o] nature has already been bringing wildlife back to the land.

Rapp/McCowin Conservation Easement, Alden

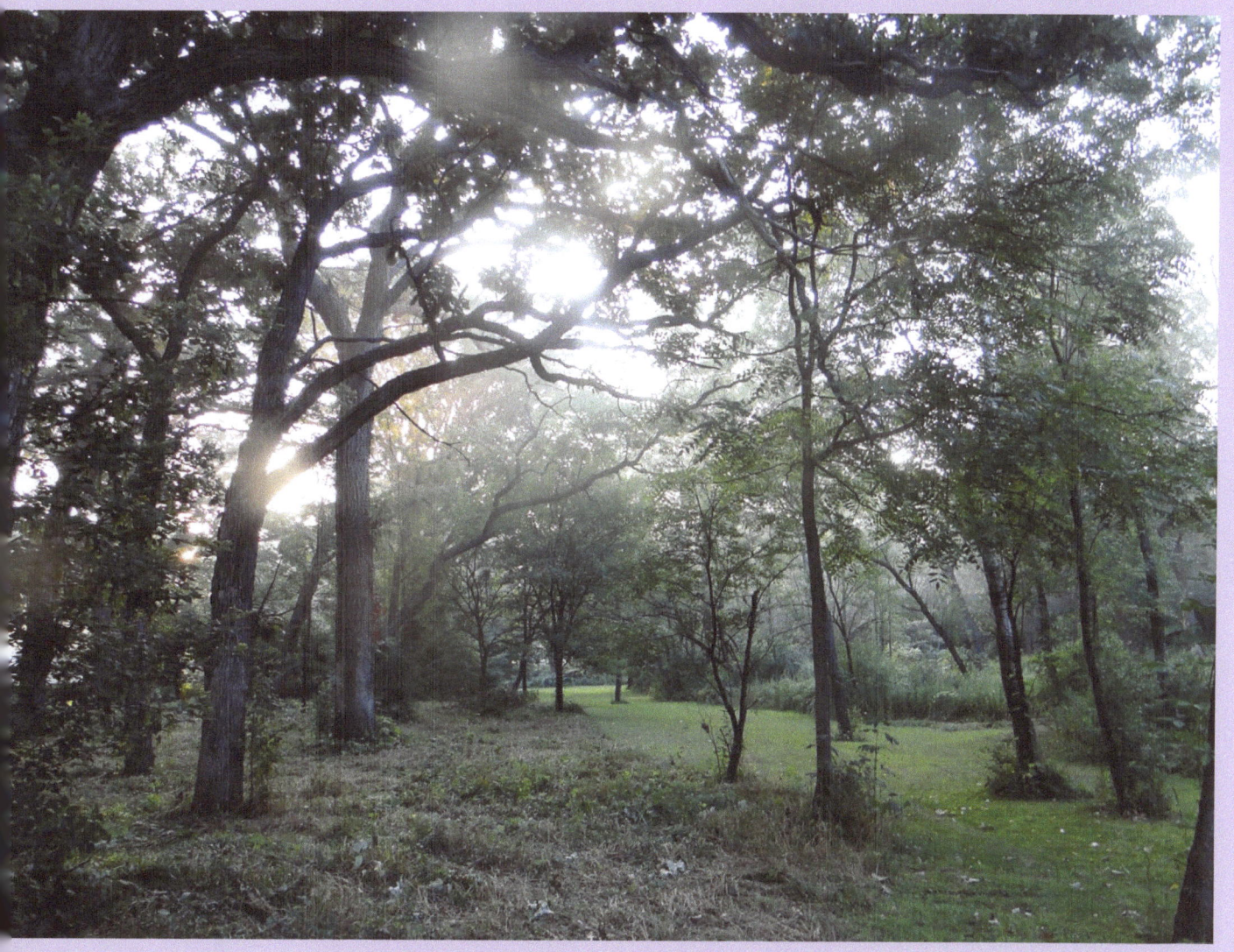

Photographer: Simon Stevens
2 Acres dedicated to TLC in 2006

A beautiful stretch of the Nippersink Creek in Alden was preserved forever thanks to an easement dedicated by Randy Rapp and Susan McCowin. Restoration of the stream bank ensures the stream and the adjacent forest will remain healthy and high quality.

Reiland Conservation Easement, McHenry
2nd Place Winner

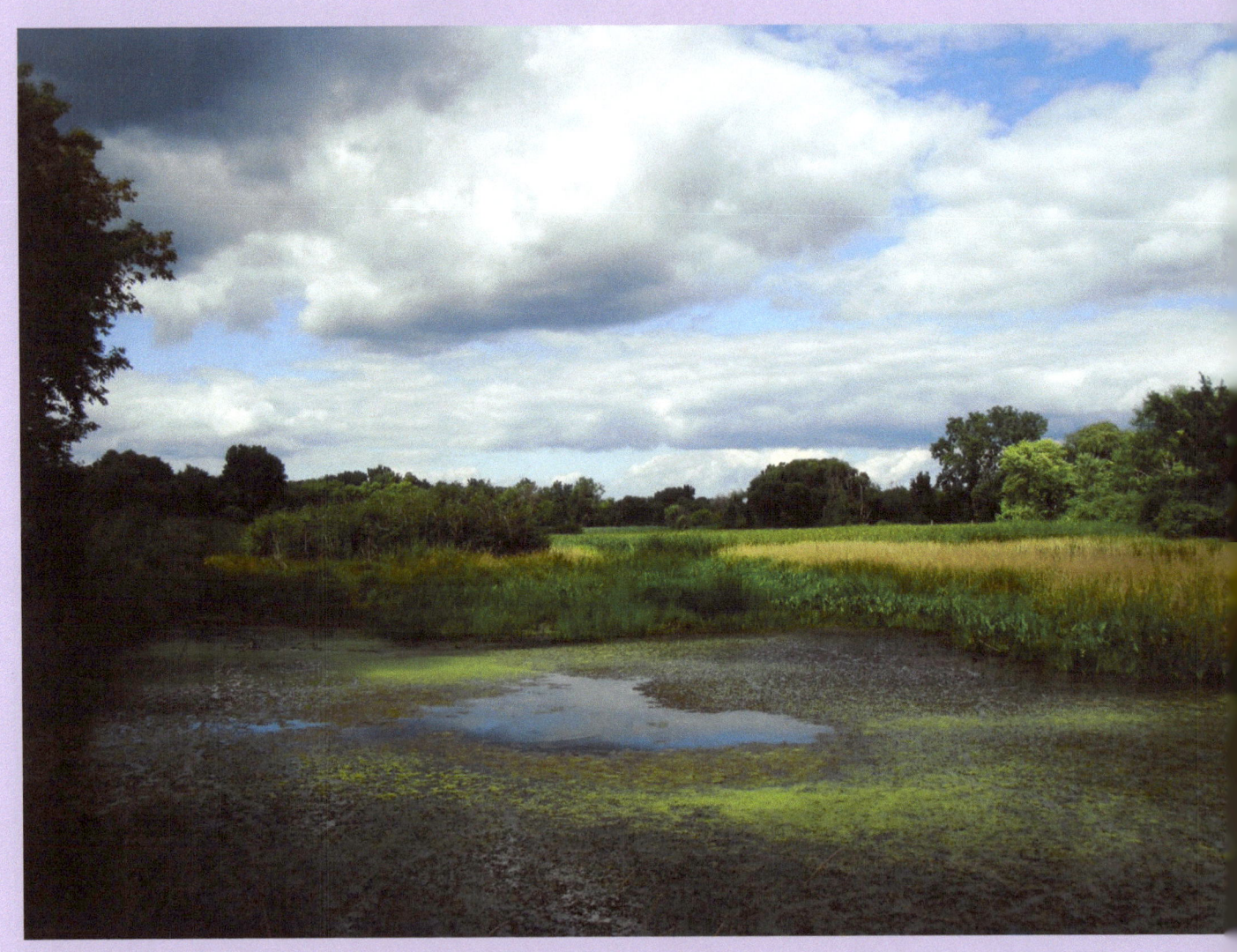

Photographer: Jerry Rygg
14 Acres dedicated to TLC in 2006

After a neighbor donated a 4 acre parcel to TLC, Kathy Reiland dedicated her 14 acre conservation easement protecting the entirety of this beaver-created wetland in perpetuity.

Robbins Conservation Easement, Hebron

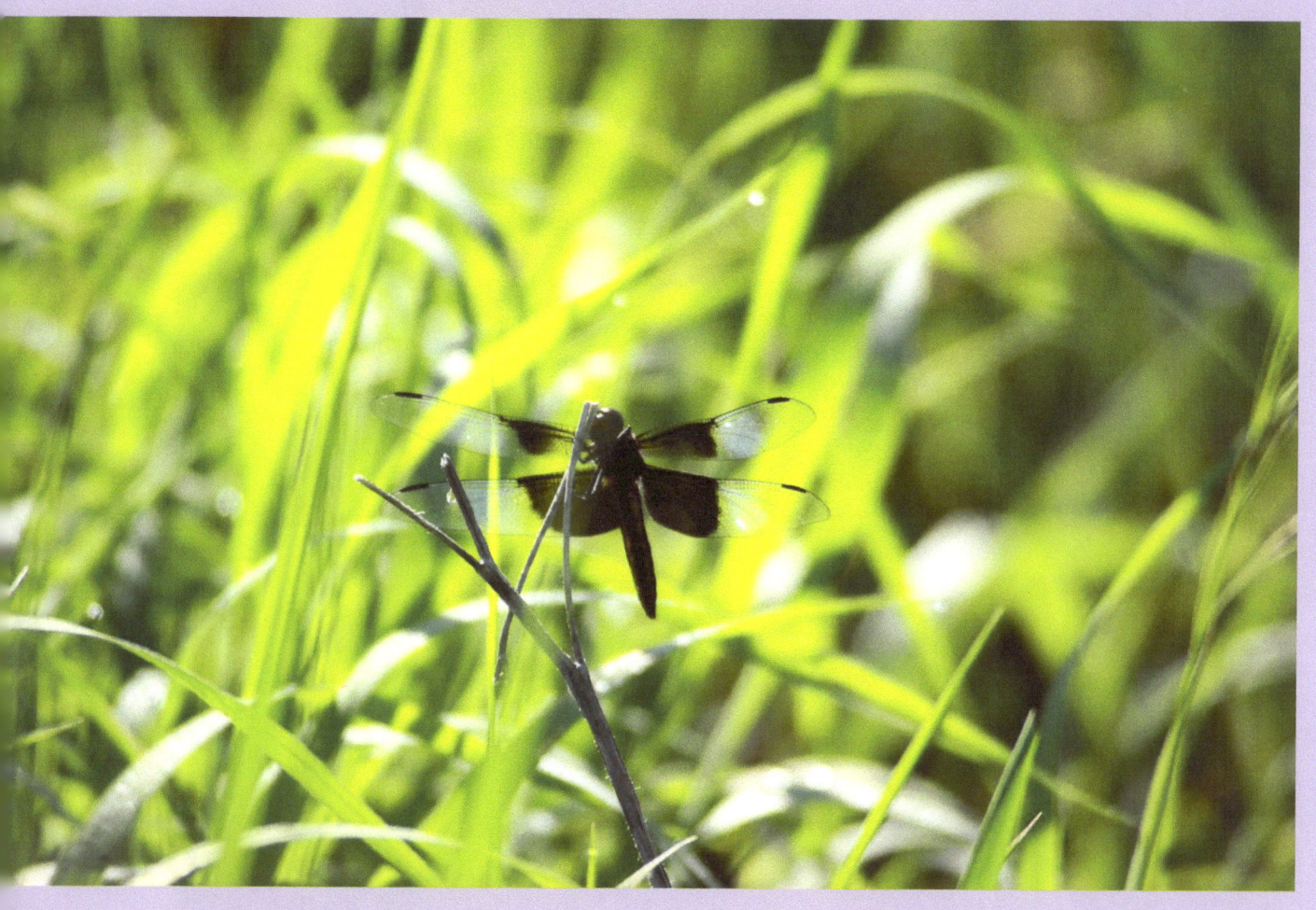

Photographer: Samantha Linhart
9 Acres dedicated to TLC in 2009

Ed and Dian Robbins have a variety of habitats, including a grove of ancient hickories, a section of the Nippersink Creek, and six and a half acres that were planted with thousands of native hardwoods.
Over time the property will become a woodland on the banks of Nippersink Creek.

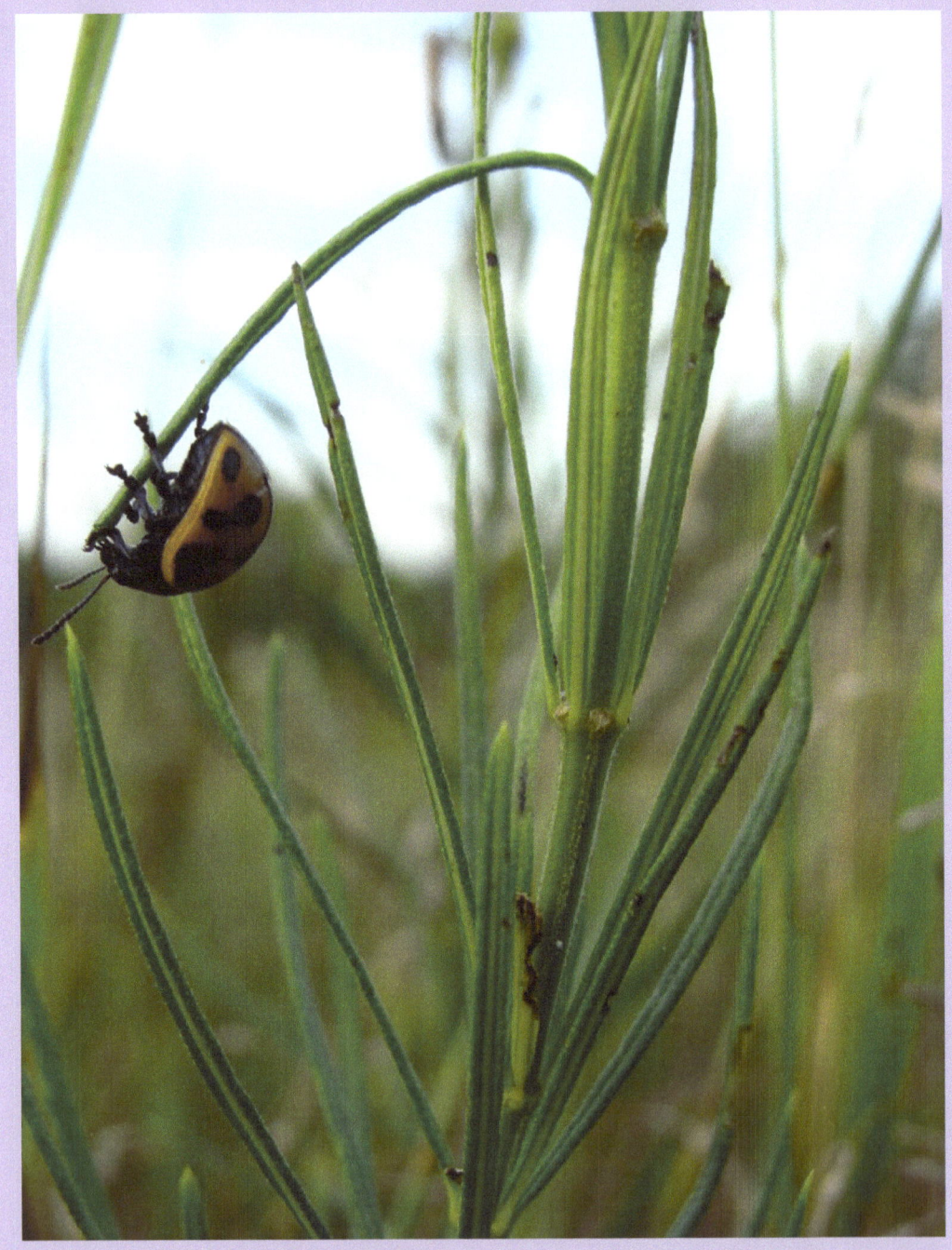

Photographer: Sue Boettcher
1 Acre dedicated to TLC in 2007

Stephanie Shetler-Simon and Jerry Simon acquired a beautiful stretch of land with the Nippersink Creek running through it. The rolling topography offers a spectacular view of the creek and all the wildflowers blooming along it--thanks to many hours of hard work!

Swanson Conservation Easement, Ringwood

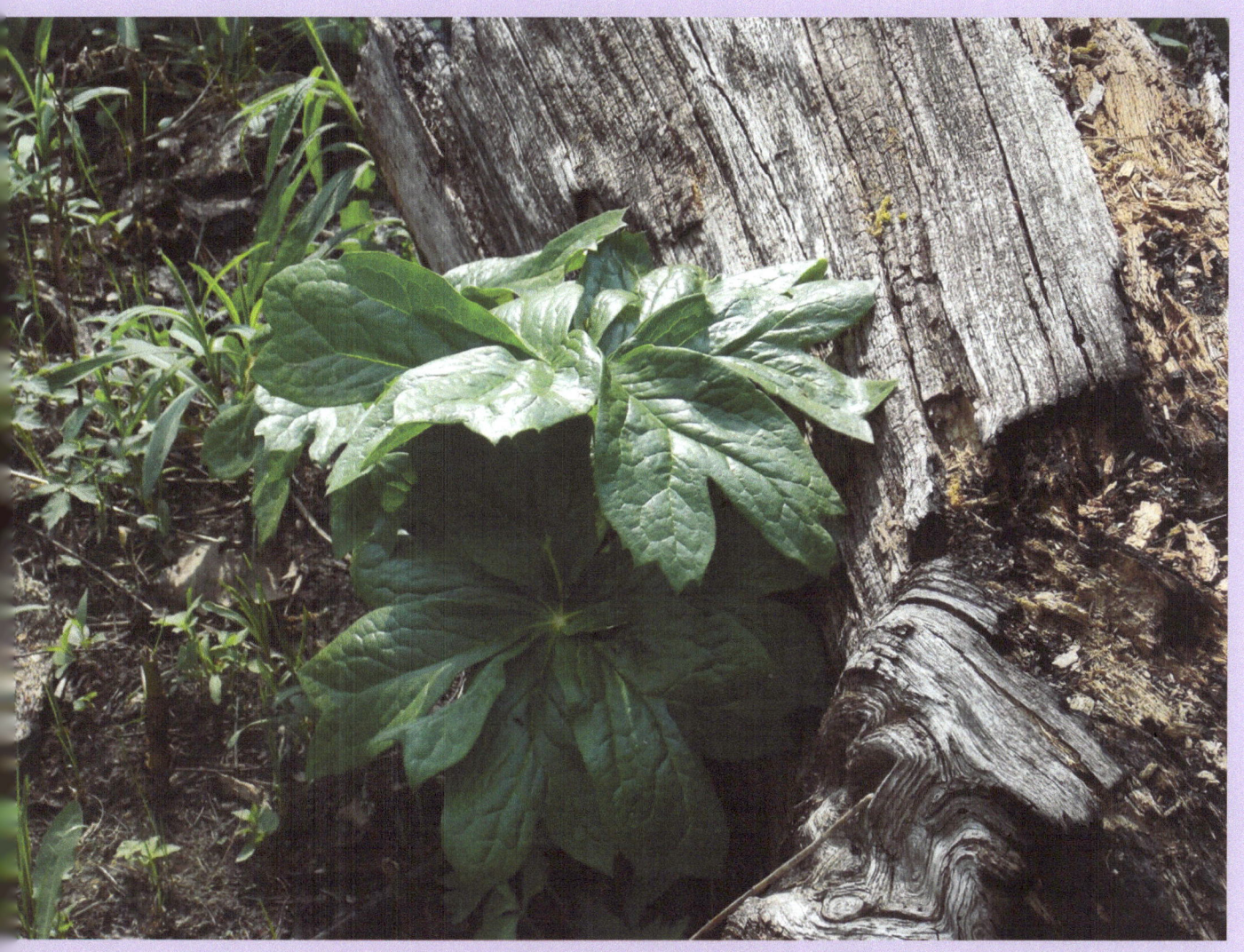

Photographer: Patty Magierski
4 Acres dedicated to TLC in 2009

Walking paths wind through groves of oak trees and around ponds, offering an astounding view of various wildflowers in all seasons. Even the smallest areas of land can host a grand diversity of plants and animals. Few backyards can boast the amount of songbirds, frogs and other critters that call this their home. Thanks to years of careful tending by Marti and Ken and the foresight to dedicate an easement, this backyard will remain natural in perpetuity.

Tagatz Conservation Easement, Bull Valley

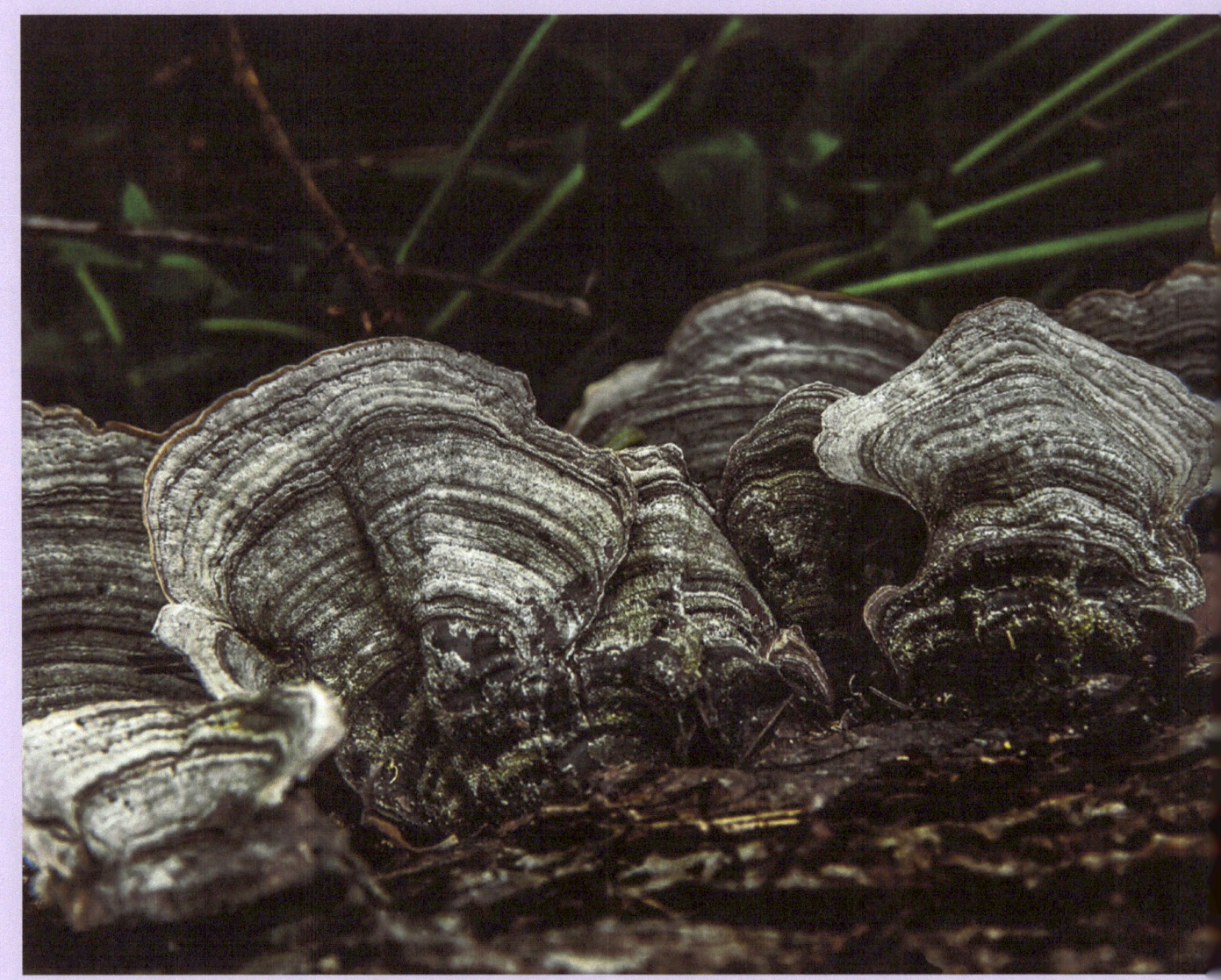

Photographer: Karen Gallwitz
3 Acres dedicated to TLC in 2008

This three acre parcel of ancient oak woodland lies in the heart of one
of the largest remaining oak woodlands in McHenry County.
Wildflowers of all shapes and sizes thrive in the understory.

Tagatz Conservation Easement, Bull Valley

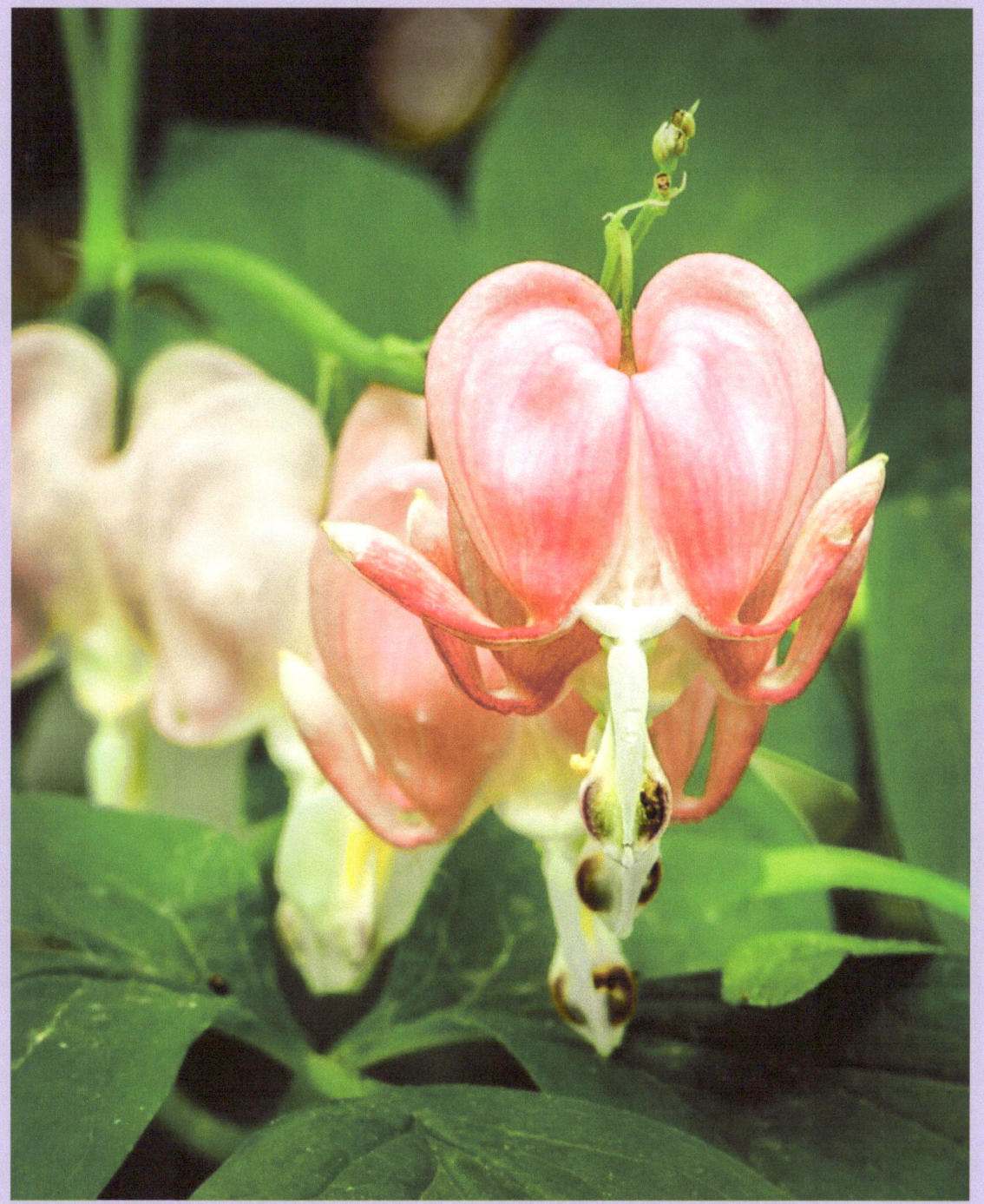

Photographer: Nancy Strahinic
3 Acres dedicated in 2008

Brian Tagatz has spent many hours planting oaks and patches of prairie to ensure that this piece of nature will remain intact for future generations.

Tauck Conservation Easement, Seneca Township

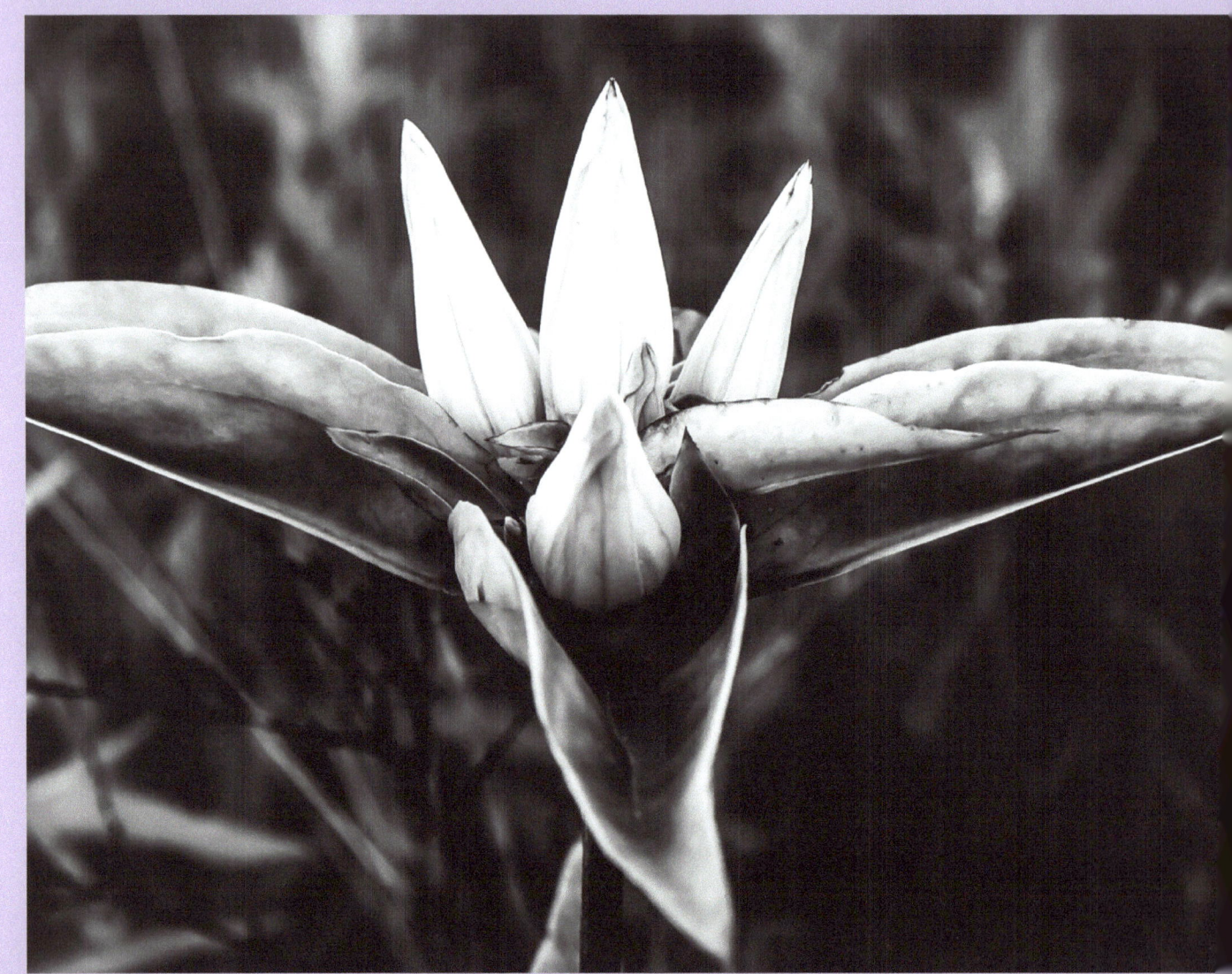

Photographer: Lisa Davids
61 Acres dedicated to TLC in 2004

In the forty years Susan Tauck has lived on the property, she has been watching the native flora and fauna. The woodland and vernal pools of the easement have the most unusual plants, and the old horse and sheep pastures are slowly turning into an beautiful prairie.

Tauck Conservation Easement, Seneca Township

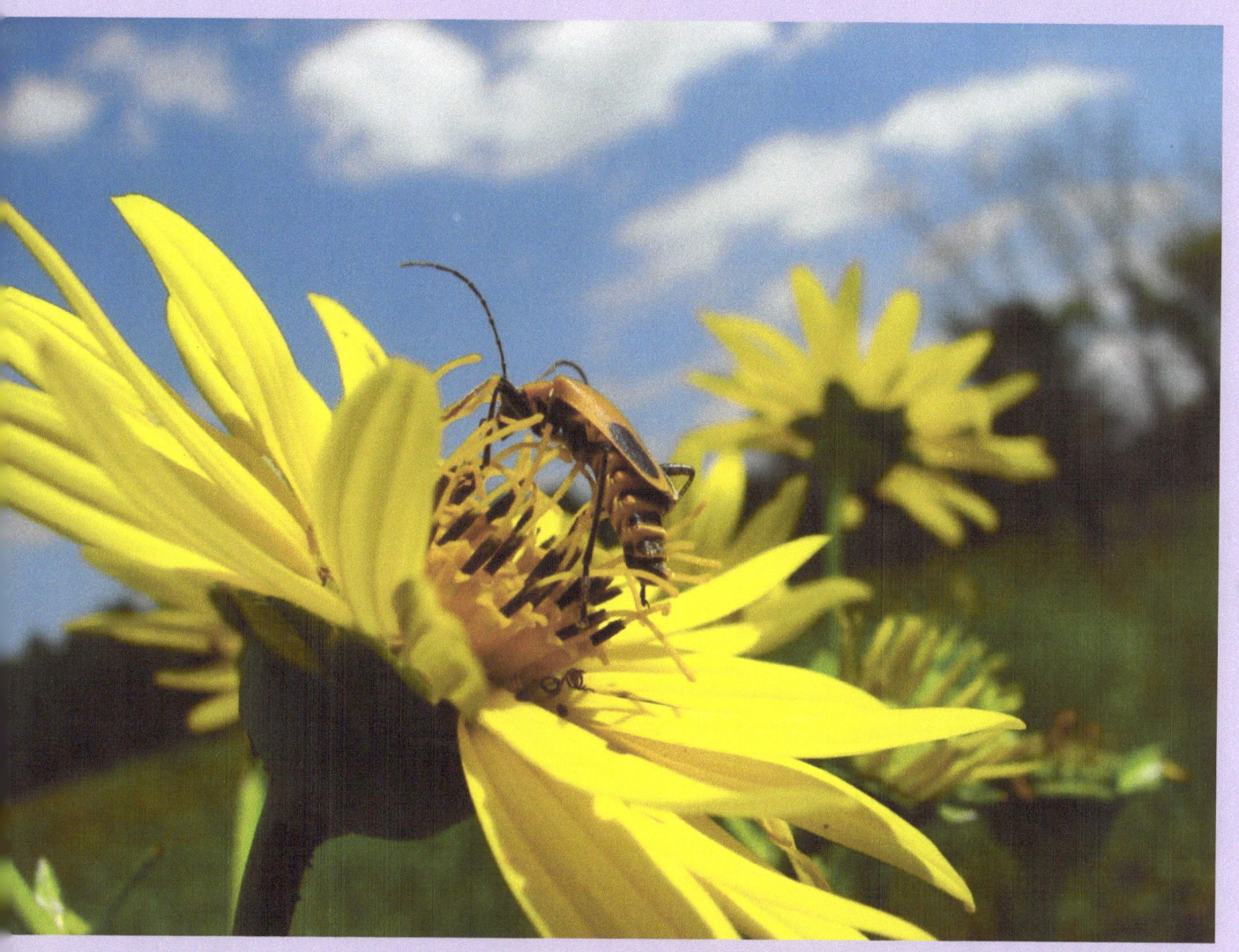

Photographer: Sarah Miller
61 Acres dedicated to TLC in 2004

Why is this place special? In Susan's own words: "Each season holds old favorites and new surprises… and each succeeding year the woodland acres and the prairie restoration portion improves. As an old nature lover, it is a comfort to know that the 60+ acres of native species in the easement will continue to flourish."

Waichunas Wetland Conservation Area, Nunda Township

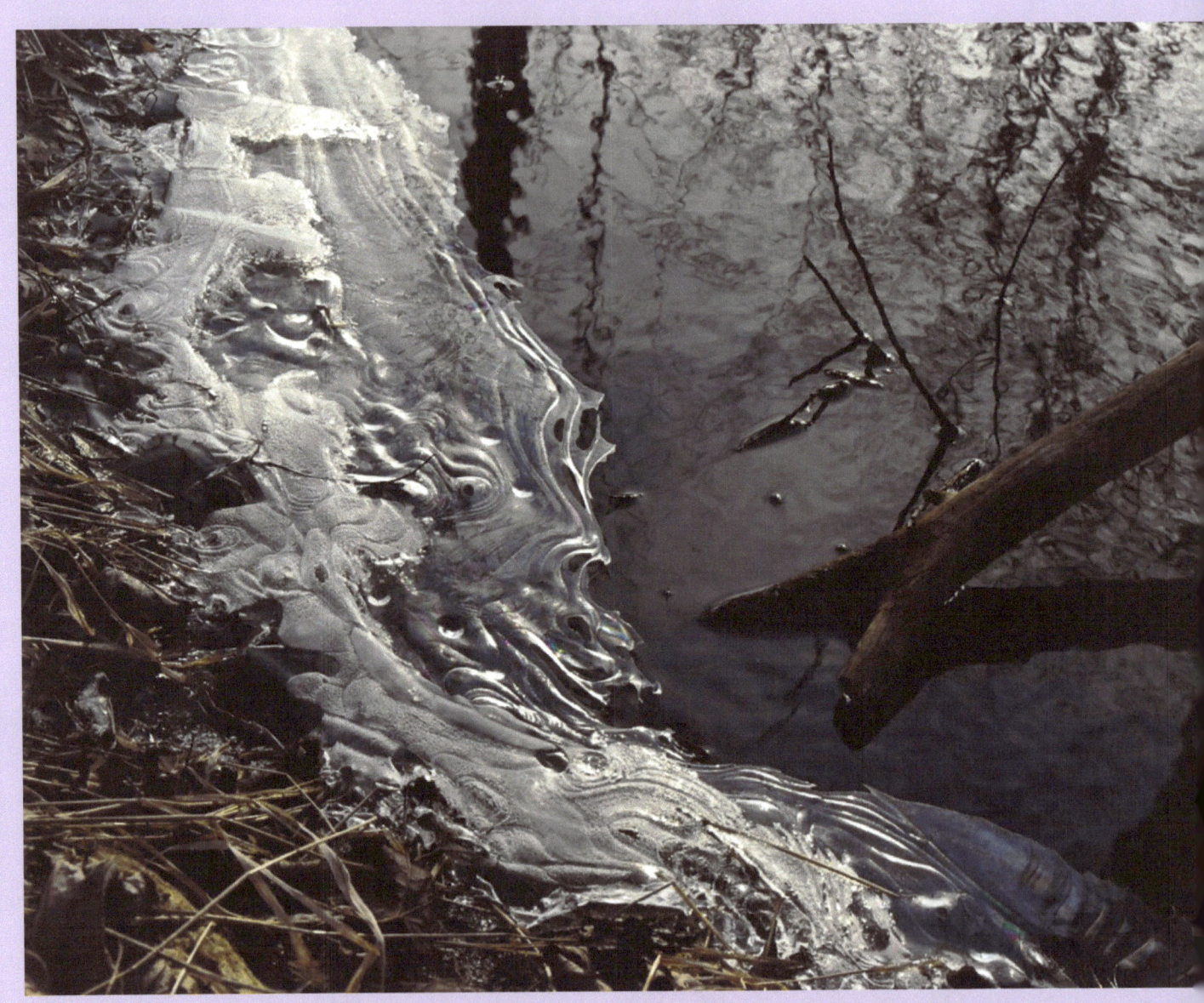

Photographer: Margie Bjorkman
4 Acres donated to TLC in 2002

During a 1997 survey, the Griswold Prairie area was identified as one of only a few remaining unprotected high quality natural areas in McHenry County. Peter Waichunas decided to donate this land to The Land Conservancy, protecting an area for Red-headed Woodpeckers--a declining species.

Weier-Zoost Conservation Area, Island Lake

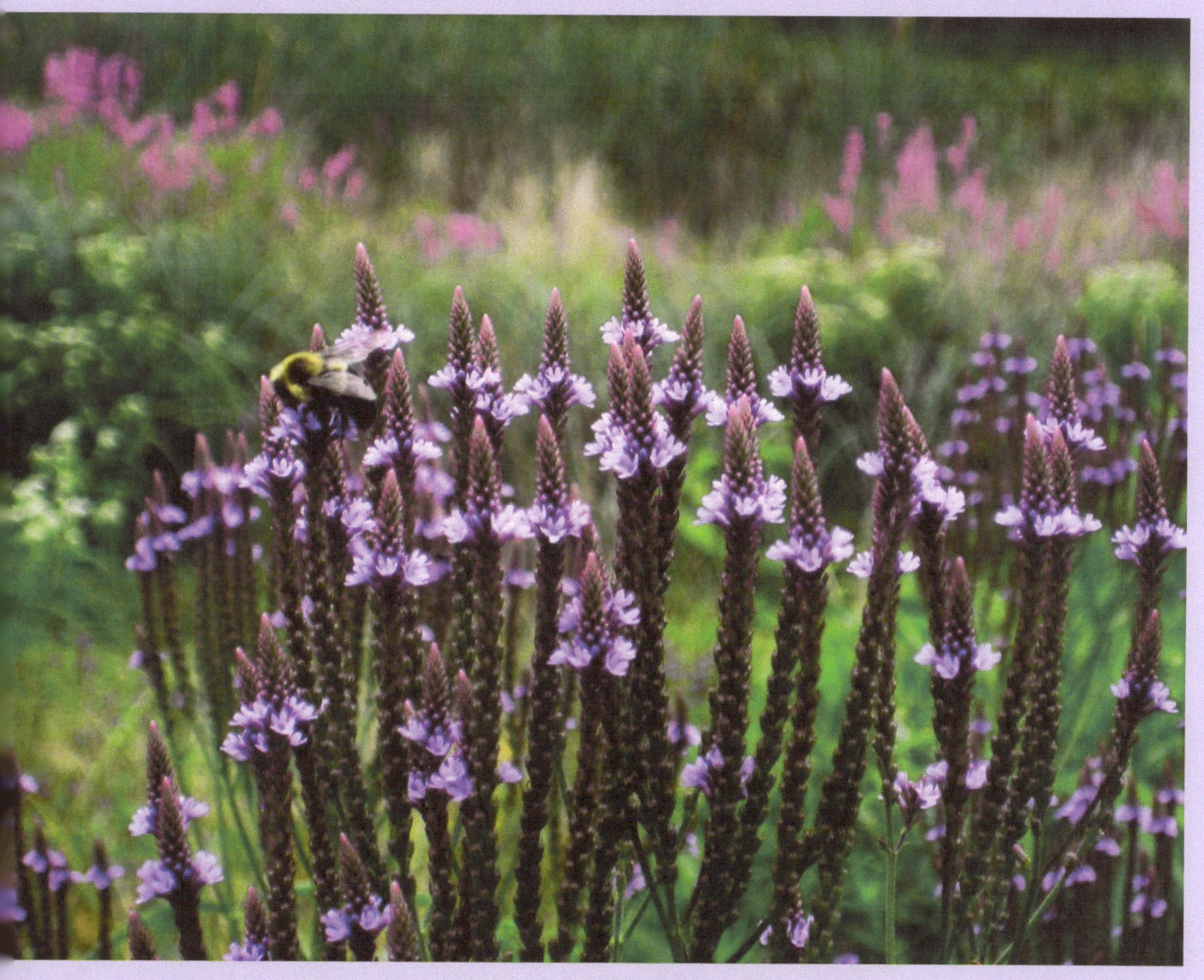

Photographer: Diane Rietveld
4 Acres donated to TLC in 2011 and 2012

Carol and Matthew Zoost donated this parcel that includes oak woods and sedge meadow, providing wildlife habitat and visual appeal to people passing by on Roberts Road.

Westwood Conservation Area, Woodstock

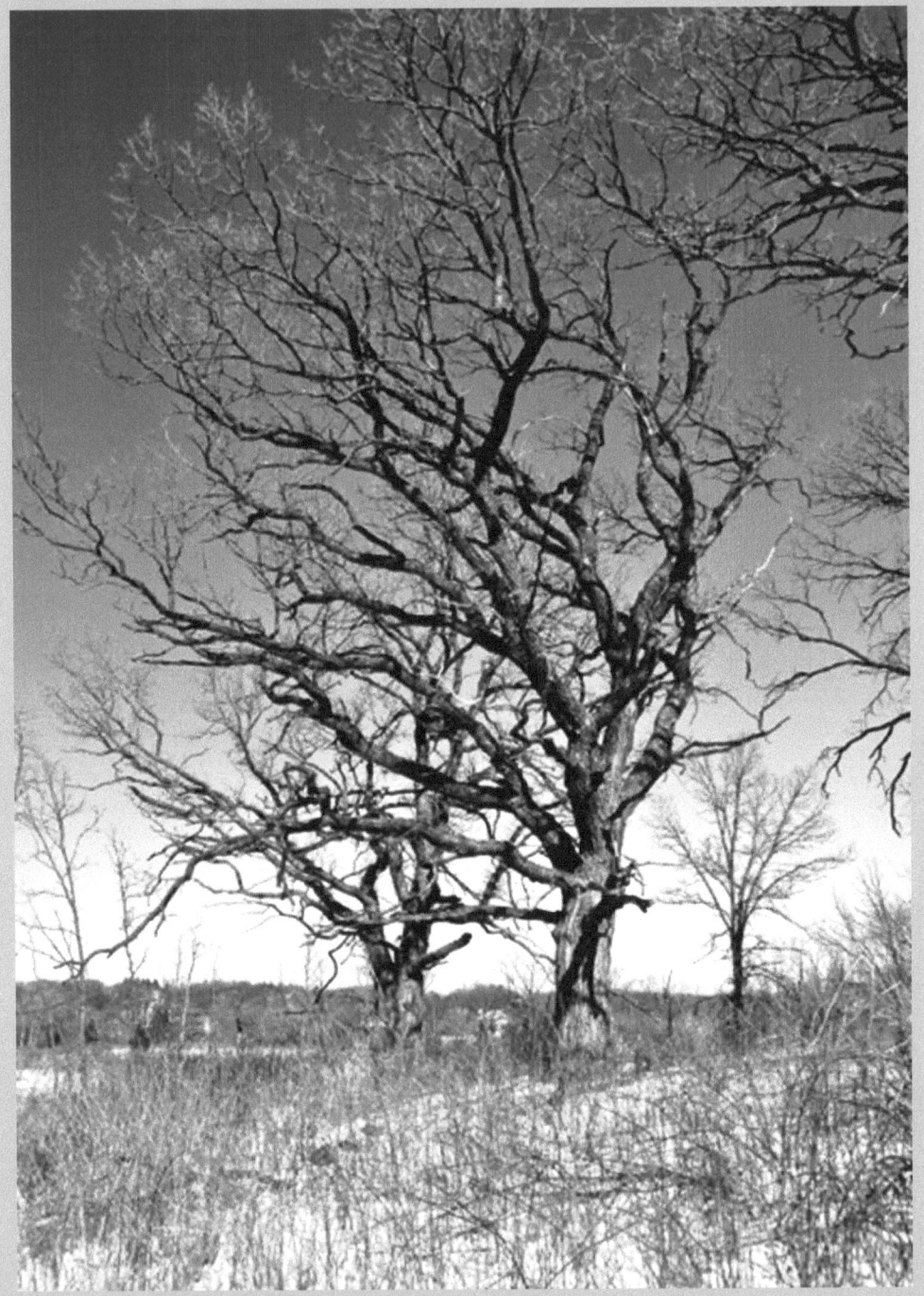

Photographer: Mindy Moister
63 acres owned by the City of Woodstock, managed by
TLC since 2006

In 2010, this property was dedicated as an Illinois Nature Preserve ar
buffer for the adjacent TLC Yonder Prairie. Restoration work has bee
underway for several years opening up the woodland full of massive
oaks, and working along the edge to let it gently grade into the prairi

Wicker Conservation Easement, Alden
1st Place Winner

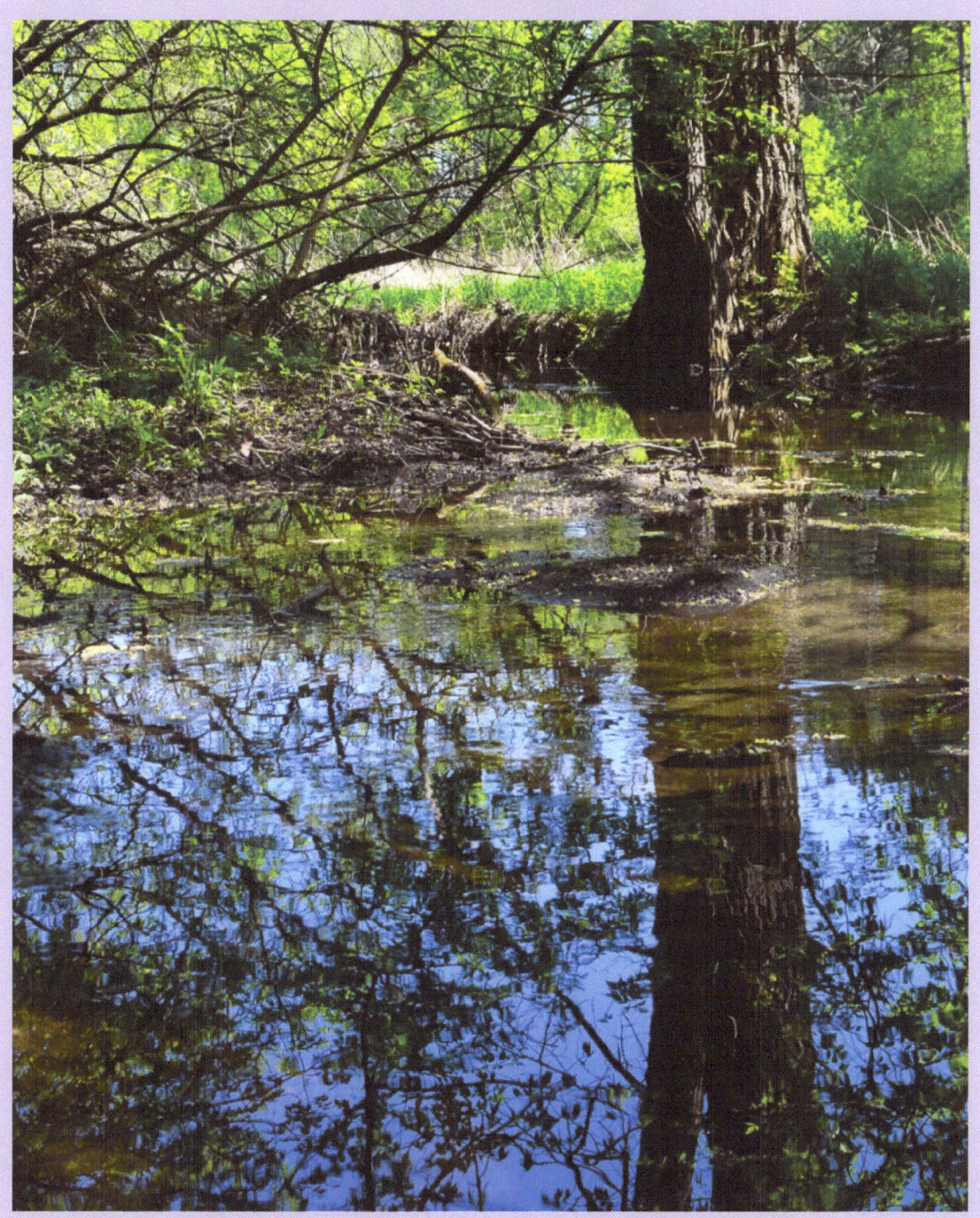

Photographer: Jon Hellmann
14 Acres dedicated to TLC in 2003

Nancy Wicker had the goal of fostering abused or neglected horses, but also cared for the land. In 2001, she enrolled her property into the USDA's Wildlife Habitat Improvement Program, planted hundreds of native shrubs, and restored the wetland areas.

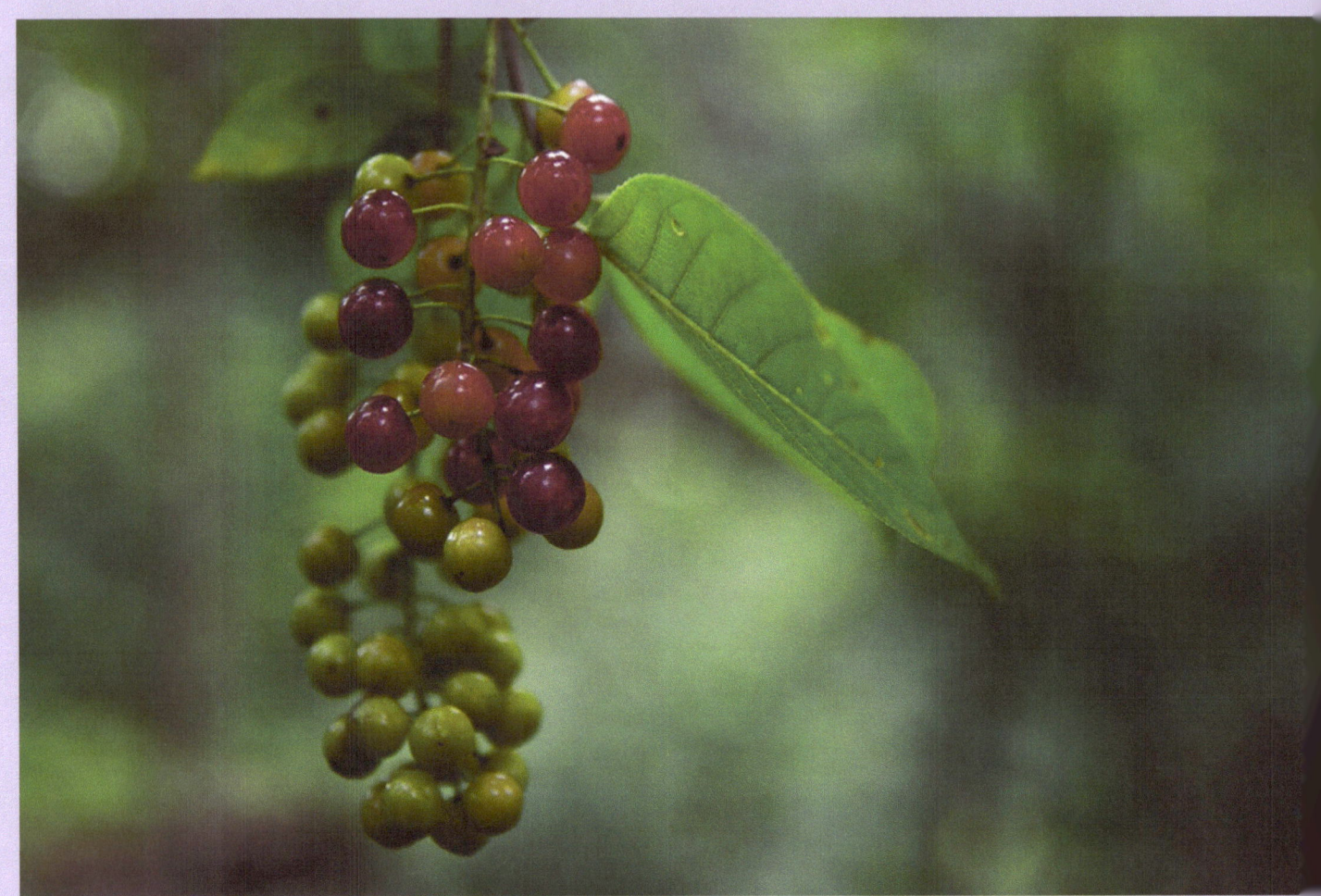

Photographer: Maggie Hay
2 Acres dedicated to TLC in 1999

You might not think "nature" when in this densely populated area of the county, where strip malls, subdivisions, and roads abound. But in this back yard you'll find oaks, wildflowers, deer, and birds, just as they were centuries ago!

Wilson Conservation Easement, Lake in the Hills

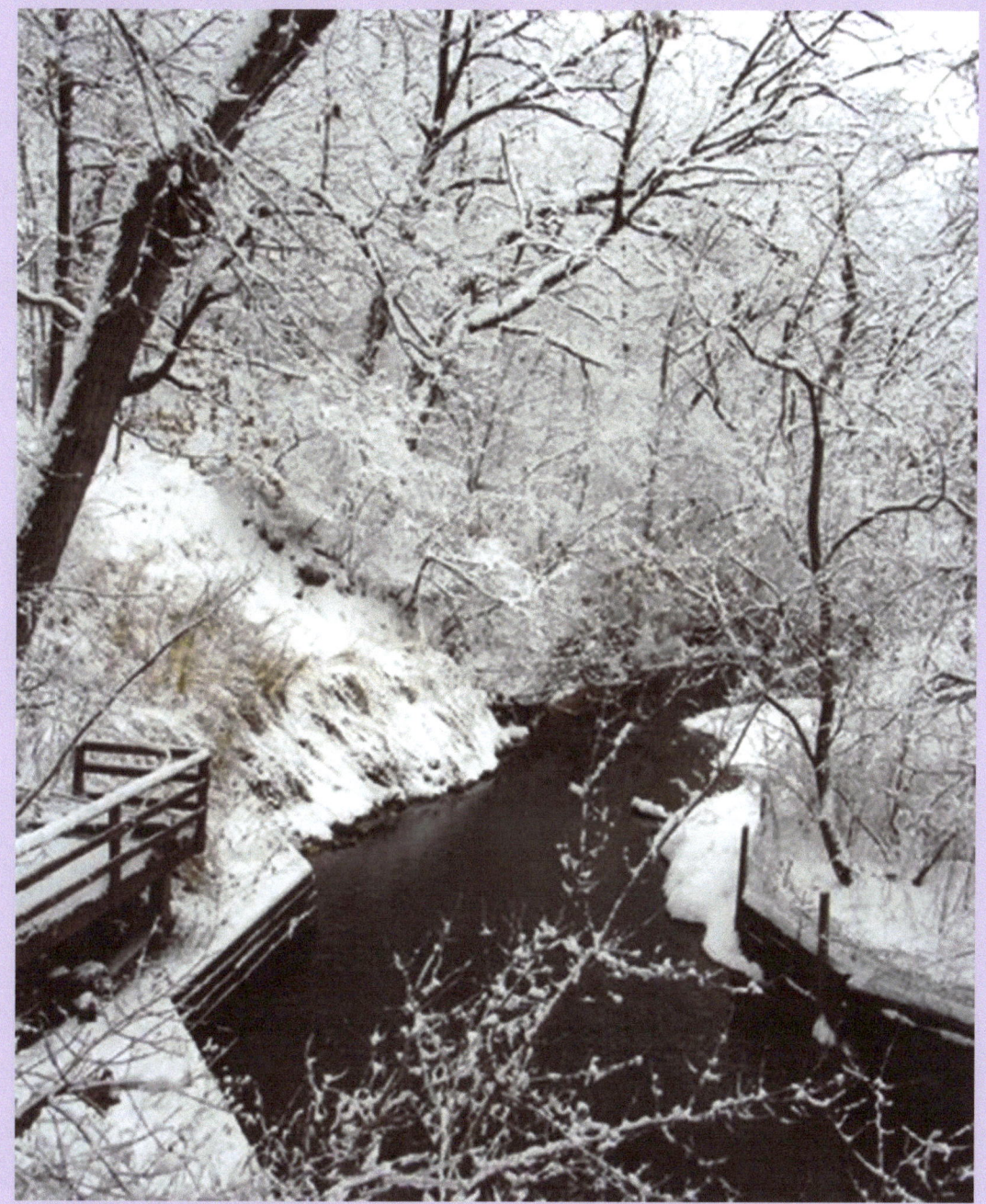

Photographer: Harris Wishnick
2 Acres dedicated to TLC in 1999

Barb and Al Wilson have lovingly tended the oak woodland on their property for many years, restoring a high level of biodiversity. Woods Creek flows past their property before joining the Fox River just downstream.

Windy Knoll Conservation Area, Bull Valley

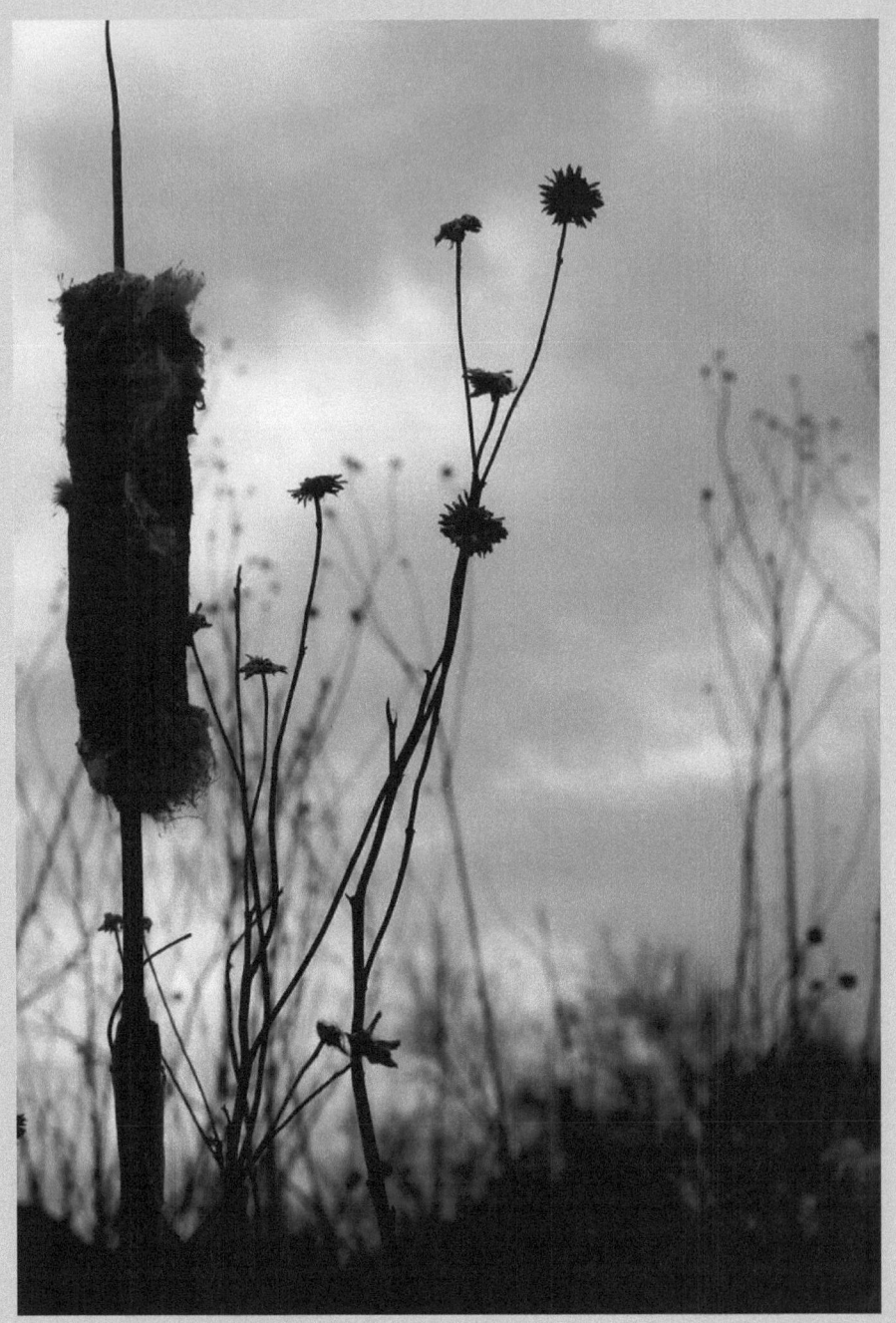

Photographer: Rinetta Dowell
22 Acres donated to TLC in 2002

TLC has held volunteer workdays here for the last 10 years. With the help of many people, we've cleared brush, added seed, and conducted prescribed burns. It's our mission to keep this parcel looking as good as it did 200 years ago!

Windy Knoll Conservation Area, Bull Valley

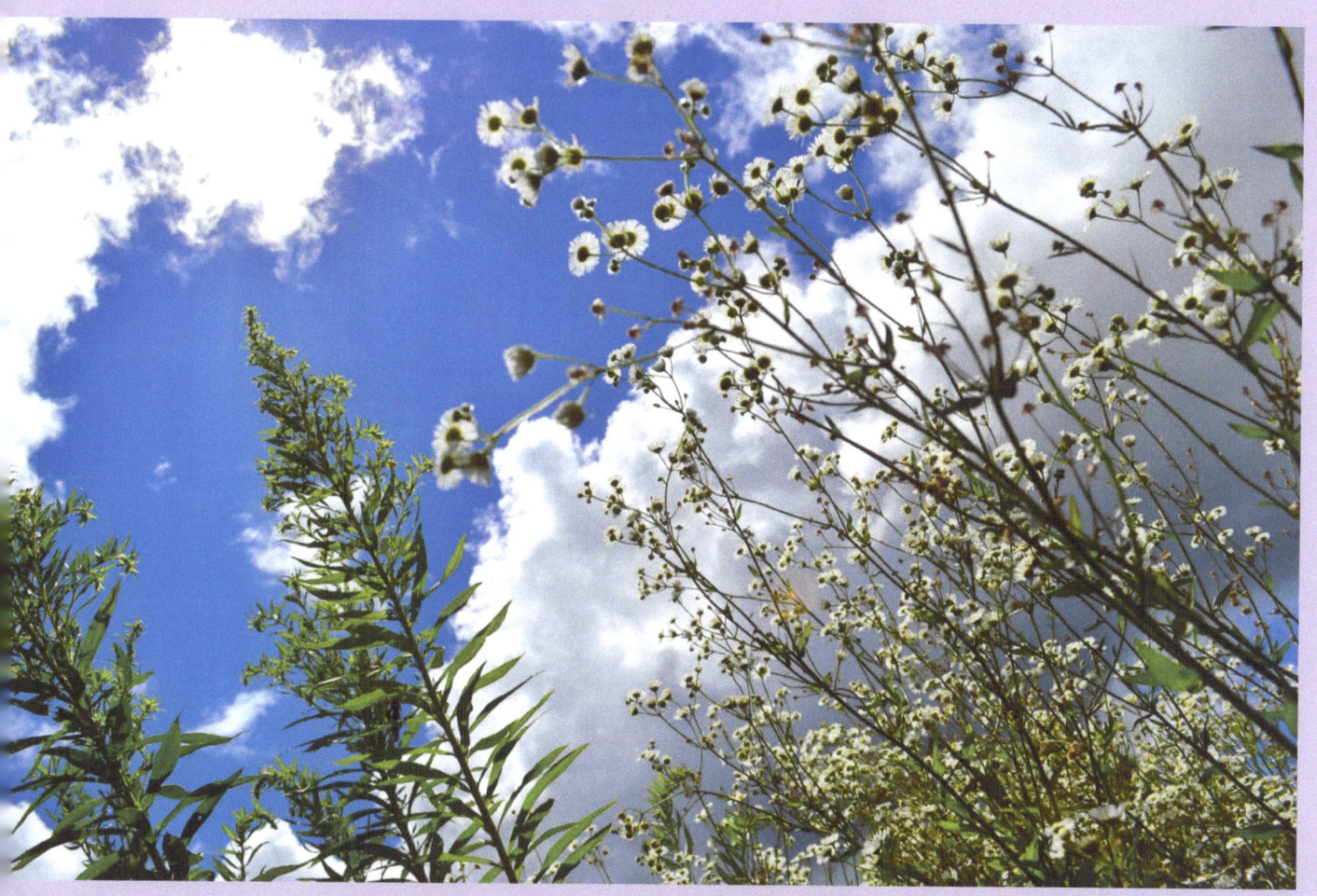

Photographer: Brittany Forgette
22 Acres donated to TLC in 2002

Windy Knoll/Powers Creek was the first land donation that TLC accepted. This is another natural area right in the middle of a subdivision, allowing residents easy access to nature just outside their front doors.

Wingate Conservation Easement, Crystal Lake
Honorable Mention

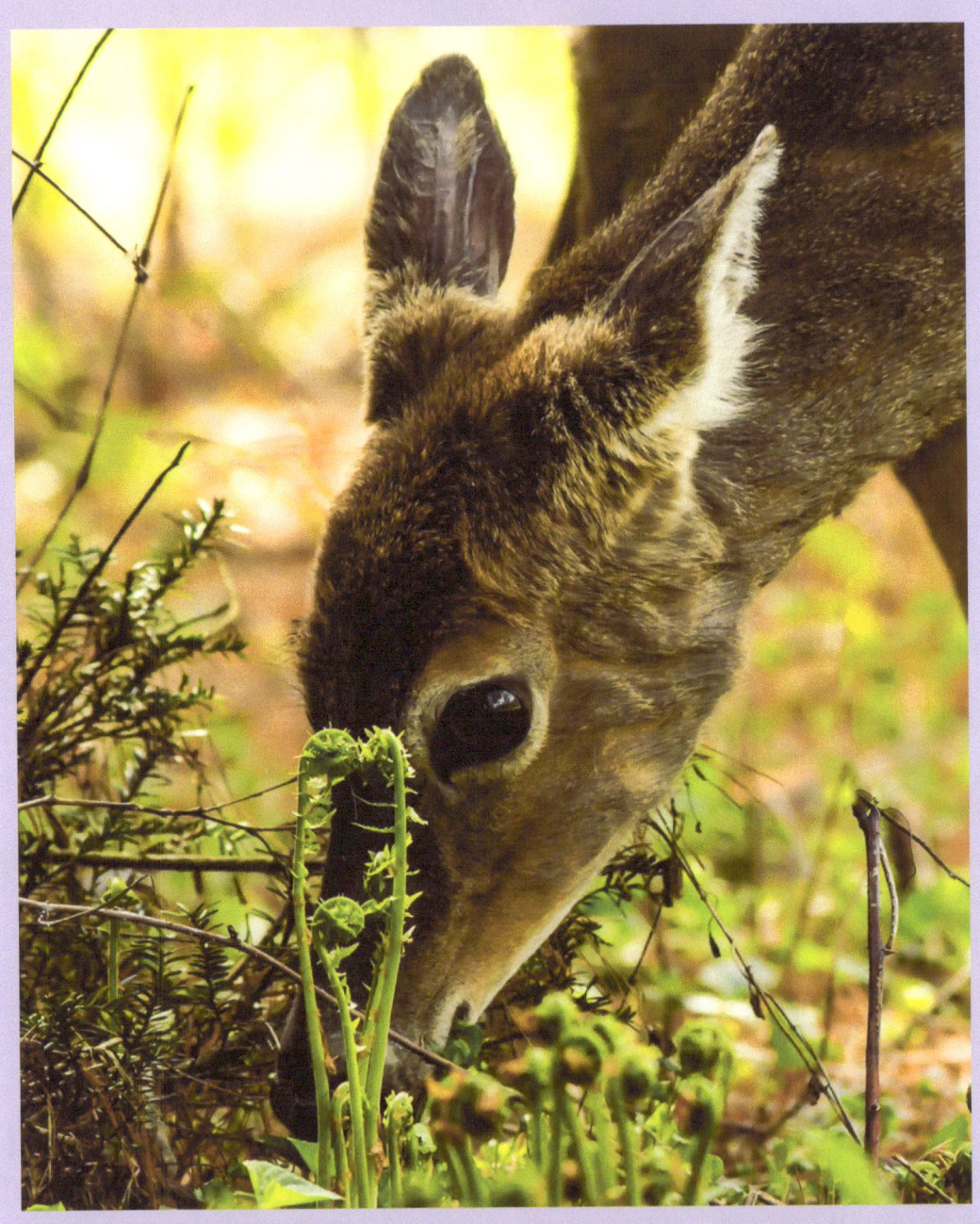

Photographer: Bob Williams
4 Acres dedicated to TLC in 1994

Bill Wingate, famous for his "Wanders with Wingate" nature walks around McHenry County, lived on this property with his wife Ardath. They transformed their backyard into a wonderful place to enjoy their own nature walks, under the trees and along a stream.

Wonder Lake Sedge Meadow, Wonder Lake

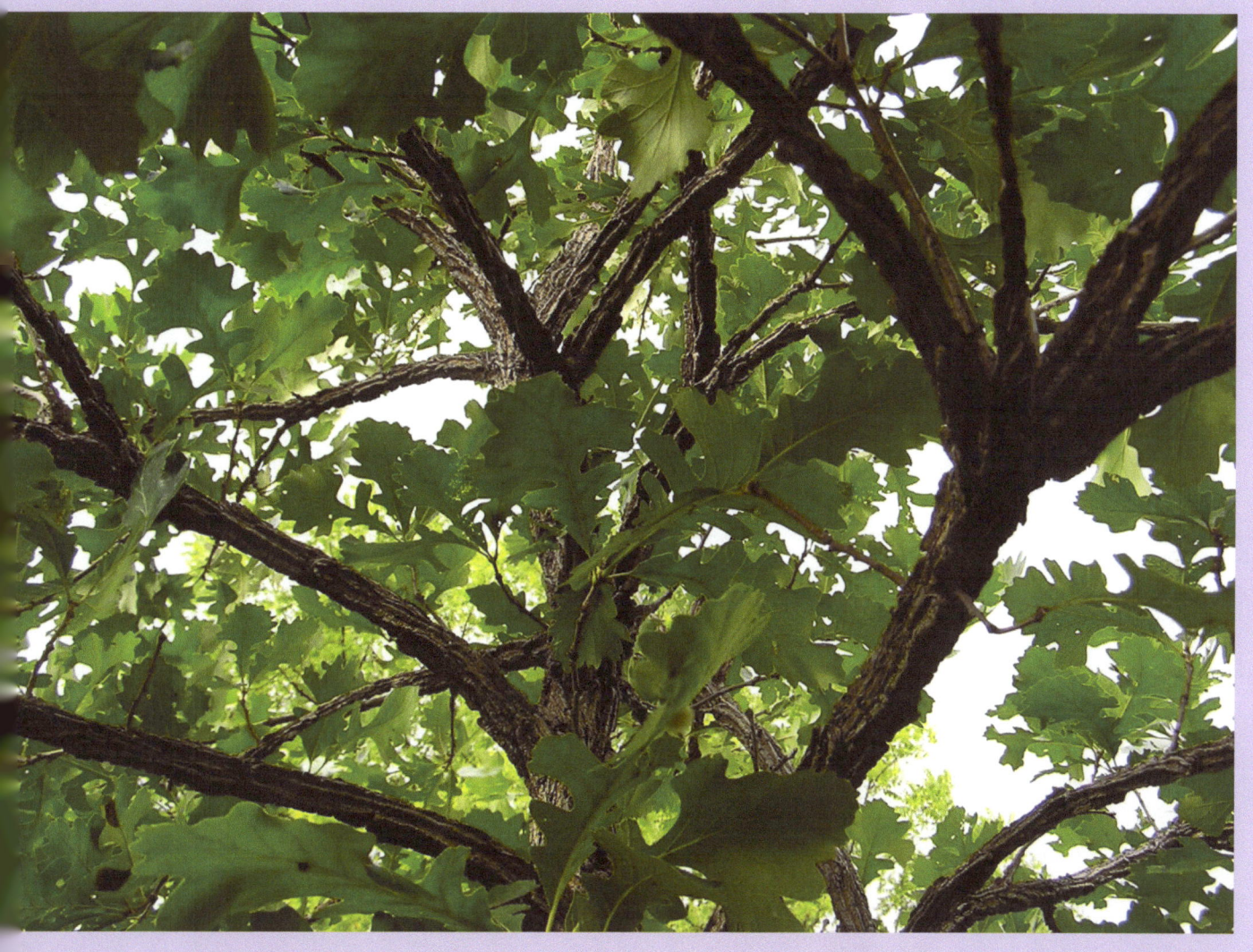

Photographer: Tracy Bordis
26 Acres dedicated to TLC in 2006

This property provides a scenic overview of sedge meadow and oak savanna, with Wonder Lake itself in the background. Thanks to the easement, generations to come will be able to stand here and enjoy the same scenic vista.

Yonder Prairie Nature Preserve, Woodstock

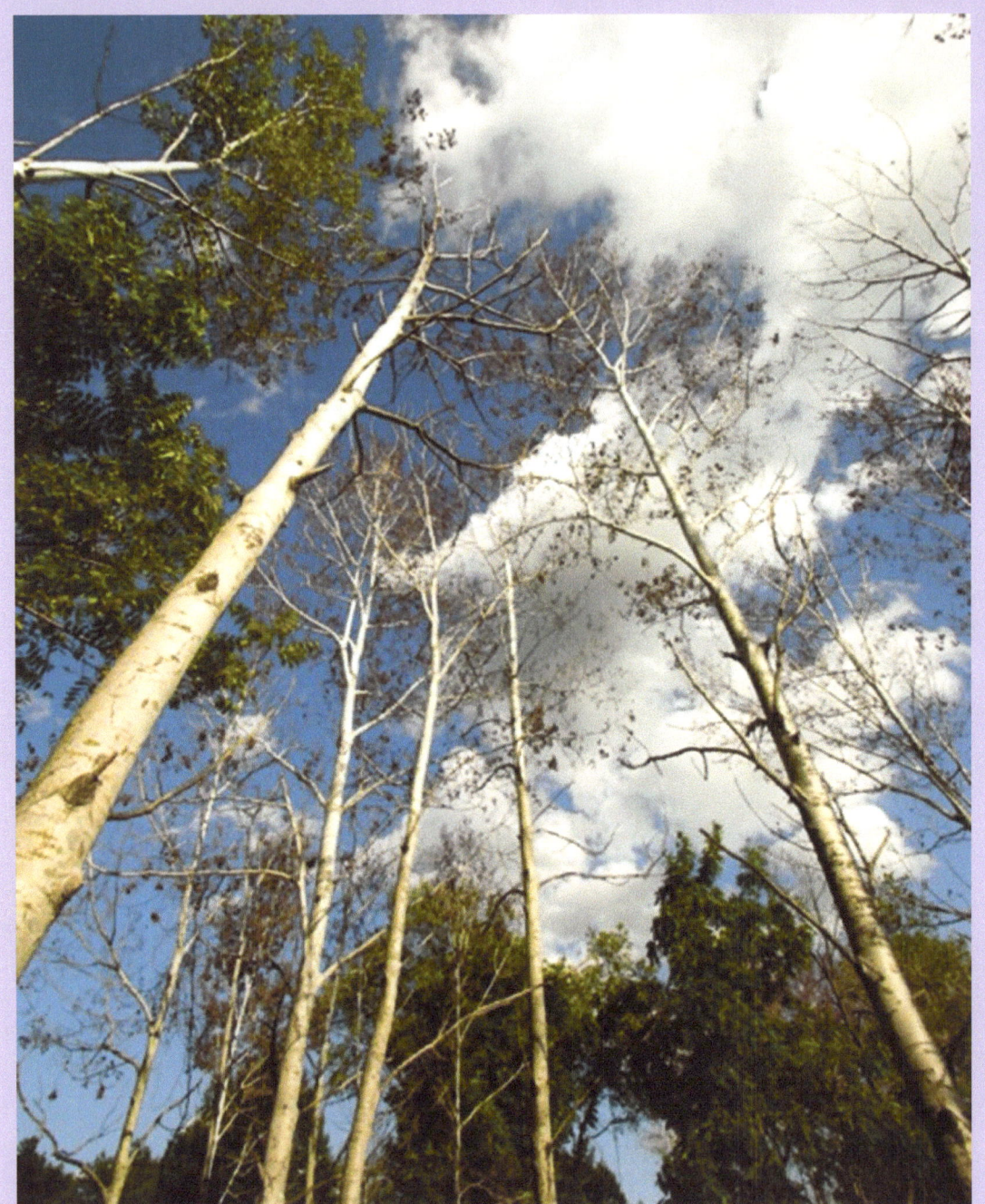

Photographer: Rand Martin
40 Acres purchased by TLC in 2008

Prior to the purchase of this land, it was deemed the highest quality unprotected natural area in the county. Now the complex of oak woodland, wet prairie and sedge meadow is classified as an Illinois Nature Preserve- the highest level of protection available to natural lands in the state.

Wingate Conservation Easement, Crystal Lake
Landowner Winner

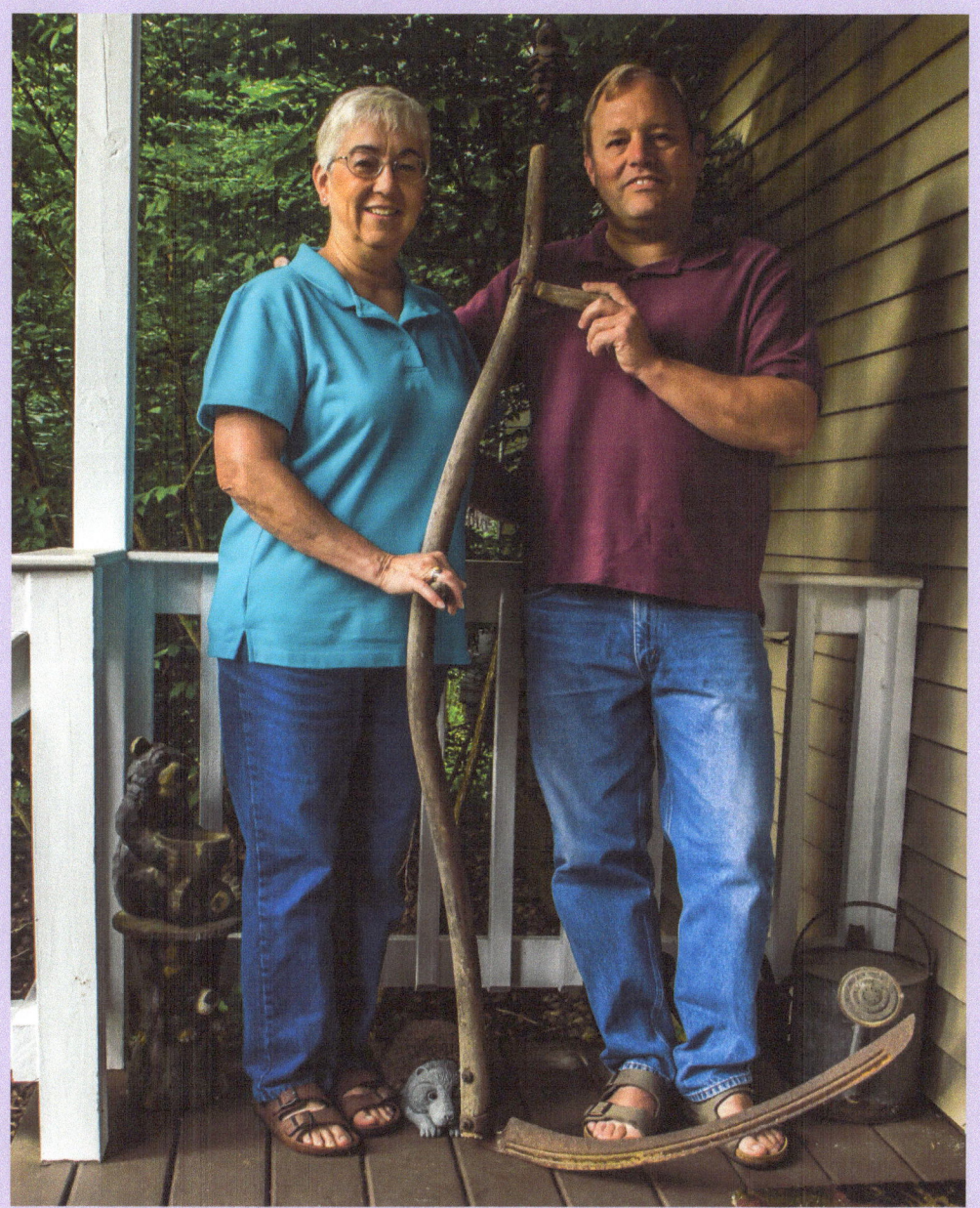

Photographer: Bob Williams
Landowners: Randy and Nancy Schietzelt

Randy and Nancy have done a phenomenal job continuing to care for the land that Bill Wingate tended. Nancy is currently the president of the Environmental Defenders of McHenry County, and Randy serves on the board for The Land Conservancy. You can usually find them putting in countless hours of work at environmental events or restoration workdays throughout the county.

Information about TLC's 2013 Art of the Land Art Sale and Benefit

2013 was the fifth year for TLC's Art of the Land Benefit at the Starline Building in Harvard. This two-night event, held in September, is a collaboration between artists from the region who find inspiration in the land and McHenry County's oldest non-profit land conservation organization: The Land Conservancy of McHenry County.

In 2013, Friday night included a special program called, "Voices of the Land," that featured conversations with local farmers and owners of natural land who talked about the future of their land once they no longer own it.

The event would not happen without the many artists who donate 30% of their sales back to TLC to support its land preservation mission, and without the hundreds of guests who attend the event and purchase artwork.

Orrin and Karen Kinney, owners of the Starline Building, donate use of the space to TLC for the benefit, and donate the labor of several workers to help set up the space for this unique show.

It's worth noting that hundreds of volunteer hours (valued at several thousand dollars), are donated during the months leading up to the event. Volunteers do everything from hanging artwork, installing lighting, painting walls, serving food, selling tickets, sweeping floors, and coordinating raffles. Quite simply, Art of the Land could not happen without the efforts of all the volunteers.

Finally, a big thank you to Holly Eberle for her help with design of this photo book.

TLC's Art of the Land Photo Contest

Each year since 2009, TLC invites amateur photographers to participate in a unique photo contest meant to highlight the inspiring nature of its land preservation work. The contest's goal is to introduce more local residents to the work of TLC and the beauty found in even small natural areas when one stops long enough to look.

TLC matches each photographer with a specific TLC property, providing them with the opportunity to visit the site throughout multiple seasons of the year. All photographs submitted are taken of properties on which TLC holds a conservation easement, land TLC owns or stewards, or of people who work with TLC for the purpose of preserving their land for the benefit of future generations.

For more information about Art of the Land, the Photo Contest, or The Land Conservancy, please visit www.ConserveMC.org.

TLC's 2013 Photo Contest was sponsored by Behr Metal Recycling of Woodstock for the fifth straight year. Thank you!

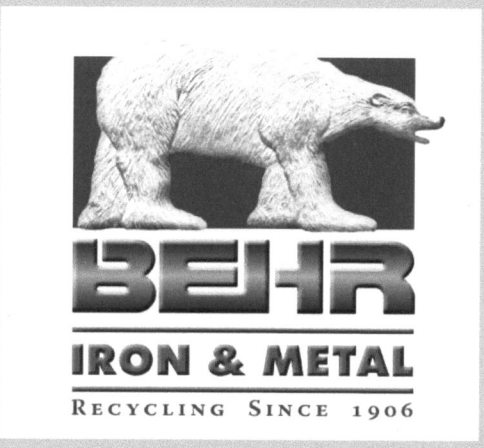

www.ingramcontent.com/pod-product-compliance
Lightning Source LLC
Chambersburg PA
CBHW050824180526
45159CB00004B/1783